The
Potter's
Guide to
Ceramic
Surfaces

The Potter's Guide to Ceramic Surfaces

JO CONNELL

krause
publications

700 E. State Street • Iola, WI 54990-0001

A Quarto Book

Copyright © 2002 Quarto Inc.

First published in the United States of America
in 2002 by Krause Publications, Iola,
Wisconsin.

**krause
publications**

700 E. State Street • Iola, WI 54990-0001

700 East State St., Iola, WI 54990-0001
Telephone 715-445-2214

Please call or write for our free catalog of
publications. Our toll-free number to place an
order or obtain a catalog is 800-258-0929.

ISBN 0-87349-359-1

Library of Congress Catalog
Card No. 2001095626

QUAR.CDT

This book was conceived, designed, and
produced by Quarto Publishing plc
The Old Brewery
6 Blundell Street
London N7 9BH

Project Editor Tracie Lee Davis
Art Editor Sally Bond
Assistant Art Director Penny Cobb
Copy Editor Mary Senechal
Designer Bill Mason
Photographer Ian Howes
Proofreader Anne Plume
Indexer Dorothy Frame

Art Director Moira Clinch
Publisher Piers Spence

Manufactured by Universal Graphics
Pte Ltd., Singapore
Printed by Leefung-Asco Printers
Trading Ltd., China

9 8 7 6 5 4 3 2 1

Contents

CHAPTER 2
TECHNIQUES USED AT THE BISCUIT STAGE

CHAPTER 3
ALTERNATIVE FIRING TECHNIQUES

CHAPTER 4
MULTIPLE FIRINGS AND POST-FIRING TECHNIQUES

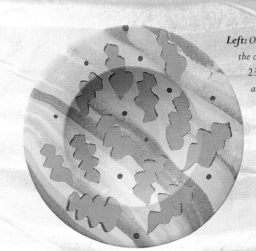

Left: Oak-leaf bowl by Jo Connell, using the clay appliqué method (see page 23). The bowl was press-molded and joined to make a hollow form.

Above: Paper-clay form by Ruth Lyne. Paper clay was painted thickly onto coarse, open-weave hessian, biscuit fired, and then raku fired.

Introduction

FOR MANY YEARS I have taught ceramics to a wide range of people, some of whom could spare only a couple of hours a week to focus on the subject. There is a particular problem that often develops in this situation—I term it the "blank canvas syndrome." The student naturally concentrates on the making of a clay object. Of course, this appears to be the first and most obvious step—and coiled, slabbed, pinched, and thrown pots emerge biscuit fired from the kiln several weeks later. Then the inevitable "next step" must be faced. It is fear of this next step that accounts for the large number of biscuit-fired pots remaining unclaimed on the shelves of every college pottery studio at the end of each year! Fear of ruining a good pot with poor decoration or a miserable glaze, or even simple indecision, can often halt a pot at this stage until it gathers dust and eventually finds its way to the trash can.

As a first-hand sufferer of blank canvas syndrome, I have gradually come to understand more about surface decoration. It is, of course, a highly personal thing, and we need to develop our own visual language alongside technical skills and a knowledge of ceramic materials and processes. A visual language evolves from personal experience—what we observe and investigate, what we learn and what we love, how our achievements are received by others, and so on. And this process needs to be nurtured.

A decoration or surface embellishment should not be an afterthought. Luck may play a part from time to time and is certainly part of the learning process—the happy accident is something all potters would like to happen as their work develops. Successful work of a professional nature comes from consideration of form and surface as a whole. A deeper understanding of ceramic processes and materials, coupled with a visual awareness, will eventually bring about a harmonious blend.

This book is about ceramic surfaces—decorative, functional, subtle, bold and bizarre, safe and adventurous, traditional and new. All of the techniques for producing these myriad effects have a place in the world of clay, along with many more for which there was insufficient space! The following pages are dedicated to all potters who have suffered from blank canvas syndrome. It is intended to inform, and to spark off ideas that can develop into something wonderful.

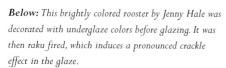

Below: This brightly colored rooster by Jenny Hale was decorated with underglaze colors before glazing. It was then raku fired, which induces a pronounced crackle effect in the glaze.

6

The surface of ceramics ranges from smooth shiny white to coarse-textured matte black, and in between there is a rainbow of colors and myriad tactile qualities. The very nature of clay as a raw material invites the maker to engage immediately in mark making, creating impressions on the malleable surface or carefully smoothing it to a fine finish. The application of color alone encompasses a huge range of techniques, and the ceramic surface can be enhanced at many different stages throughout its journey from clay to gallery shelf.

Because of modern technology, the flourishing of studio ceramics, and the information explosion, the choice of materials and techniques for the creation of surface pattern and decoration was never greater. From subtle earth colors to the vivid and brash, from print to paint, from rough to smooth, we can have whatever we want. We can and must, however, continue to learn from the past.

As any archeologist will report, there have been potters on this planet for a very long time. The discovery of clay was of immense historical importance, and the evidence fortunately remains for us to see. Numerous and wonderful collections of ceramic artifacts exist in museums and collections all over the world, and today's potter would be wrong to ignore this legacy. Students of ceramic history will find a wealth of information and inspiration just waiting to be tapped for the enrichment of their own work.

Above: This Neolithic, painted Chinese vessel from the Yangshao culture, 2,500 B.C., is an early example of painted ceramics, using iron oxide on a buff clay.

Above: The surface of this tripod vessel (Chinese, 2,500 B.C.) is decorated by subtle impressions of cord into the soft clay and the complexity of the form demands no further enhancement.

7

ANCIENT POTS

Years of handling and making ceramics has sparked my own appreciation of ancient pots. They speak so powerfully of the past, and the very fact of their continued existence is a source of amazement. For the most part, these pieces are neither colorful nor even glazed, but they have a mysterious and transcendent quality that is endlessly fascinating.

DOMESTIC POTTERY

I also enjoy using early "country" pottery and cookware, especially the pieces that supremely fit the purpose and serve as a reminder of the link between pottery and food. In this age of microwave cooking, it is rewarding to reassert the position of ceramics in the domestic environment.

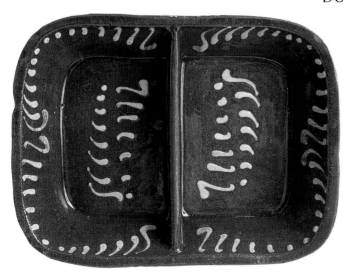

Left: A 19th-century slipware dish made in Newcastle-on-Tyne. It is divided for vegetables, and has a slip-trailed decoration. This dish was one of many produced by small country potteries throughout England. The slip-trailed decoration is simple, fluid, and direct and fits the form by defining its edges.

What is Decoration?

Ornamentation, adornment, beautification—people have always used decoration to enhance their property, their environment, and their person. Decoration is sometimes referred to in dismissive tones, as if it were some kind of superfluous, even trivial "frill," but that is to misunderstand its purpose, to underestimate its meaning and importance.

DECORATION AS NARRATIVE

Ceramic decoration was widely used in the past to reflect and celebrate daily life. Before the advent of printing and photography, ceramics played a role in recording events and spreading information. There are numerous instances of both sculptural and functional ceramics used in this way, the classical Greek vase being a perfect example. Scenes recorded on such vases are a rich and valuable source of information for historians.

Above: Historical and mythological scenes were common themes of decoration on Greek ceramics. On this vase, Hercules fights Achelous (500–475 B.C.).

Above: From a site of Roman occupation known as Manduessedum in Warwickshire, England, came this fragment of a bowl signed by its maker. Sarri.F stands for Sarrius fecit—"Sarrius made this."

DECORATION AND THE INDIVIDUAL

To decorate is also to individualize, to identify, and to express ideas. This personalization can begin as a basic signature, a stamp, or a seal—even in Roman times a stamp was used to identify the maker. The shard, left, from a site of Roman occupation shows simple decorative detail on the rim of a mortarium (a Roman mixing bowl).

DECORATION AND FASHION

Decoration can echo the contents of a vessel or its intended purpose. It can reflect its environment or the person for whom, or by whom, it was made.

Above: Highly textured by incising into the surface and by additions of clay, this piece echoes a strong African tradition.

Left: Potters today continue to stamp their work. In this piece by Peter Beard we see how the potter's stamp can be used to provide a focal point.

Right: A "Riviera," dinner plate by Midwinter, designed by Hugh Casson c.1954. This tableware decoration was sparked off by a boom in foreign travel.

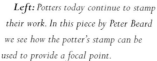

Decoration can establish traditional motifs from religion or mythology, or it can spread new ideas. The raised textural decoration in traditional African pots may echo patterns found in body scarification (*see opposite*). In 1950s Britain, a boom in foreign travel brought about a tableware design named "Riviera," depicting French cafés and fishing scenes (*see below, opposite*). Cultures, fashions, and styles have an immense influence upon the art, craft, and design of the day, and the history of ceramics clearly reflects these trends. After all, ceramic products are often domestic items, of comfortable scale, affordability, and usability. Ceramics is among the most accessible of art forms.

Above: Jug by Poole pottery. Made in the 1930s, and hand-painted with underglaze color, this piece depicts stylized floral motifs in contemporary style.

Inspiration and Individuality

The notion of inspiration as a bolt from the blue is one that I find hard to accept. Most artists have to work at it! As creative human beings we soak up, sponge-like, what is around us and become mirrors of our environment. Through the versatility of clay we can learn to express and reflect ideas and concepts that move us.

Above: Doulton vase, 1903. One of a pair by Frank A. Butler, this shows a flamboyant style of floral decoration reminding us of the popularity of Art Nouveau. At this time, "art pottery" made in the factories was decorated by artists employed specifically for that purpose.

Right: Potato bakers decorated with sgraffito. Molly Attrill finds inspiration in the heart of the farmyard in rural England where she works. She loves to draw, and uses ceramics as her canvas.

9

Right: Commemorative ware has always been made to celebrate an event, to express humor, or immortalize a statement or a portrait. This piece by Fleur Harvey uses ceramic media to preserve a collection of private memories in pictorial and narrative form.

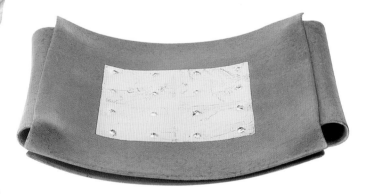

Above: Joy Bosworth finds a rich source of subject matter in the industrial West Midlands in England. We can see here an interpretation of riveted metal and machine parts in this raku-fired and smoked piece, with metal leaf applied and "distressed" to imitate surfaces she has observed.

Above and right: Color in nature inspires the potter's palette. The balance and distribution of color and its subtle diffusion is interpreted in this vessel by Jo Connell.

Right and below right: Ancient paintwork peels from this shed door, a patina of age giving it depth and character. Dawn Kyra Harbord uses textured glaze to achieve the same effect in her work.

THE VERSATILITY OF CLAY

A potter need never be stuck for subject matter, or faced with a "blank canvas." Clay itself is subject enough. Investigate the qualities of clay and it will start to behave in certain ways. Draw and paint, incise and impress, experiment with texturing, coloring, glazing, or firing—and something will happen. What will it do? How far can you push it? Through experimentation with materials and techniques, a personal vocabulary will emerge—a language both visual and tactile, from a dictionary of infinite proportions.

CLAY AS IMITATOR OF SURFACES

The multifarious ways of treating clay mean that it can be a great imitator of surfaces. It can convincingly take on the character of another material. The examples shown above and below illustrate the tactile dimension that makes clay so appealing. Pots can be handled, and they exist on an approachable, human scale. The visual qualities of ceramics are deeply satisfying, and their tactile nature increases our delight.

Left and below: It is wonderful how nature creates patterns and surfaces that are also the qualities of ceramic pieces. Here, the broken surface of a rock pool can be compared with the effect of soda glaze on this mug by Lisa Hammond. The water moves but the once liquid state of the glaze has been captured forever.

Above: Inspired by the landscape and nature, the salt-glaze potter Rosemary Cochrane has found that rutile and cobalt sponged over slips will be fluxed by the salt during the firing. The effect reminds us of the colors and patterns of lichen and mosses.

Left: Red Totem by Peter Hayes. Laminated clays are rolled onto dry porcelain so that the surface cracks. It is then burnished and fired to 1922°F (1050°C), giving the effect of old leather.

DECORATION TO FIT THE FORM

Form and surface cannot be separated. The pot and its decoration should be conceived as a whole. Decoration can accentuate form or destroy it. A subtle texture or a well-judged pattern can blend with the shape to express the character of a vessel.

Ceramicists today are working in individual ways, exploring methods of achieving particular effects, borrowing techniques and ideas from other crafts, styles, and eras, and showing great inventiveness to produce a fascinating array of exciting work. This book is intended to encourage and advance those aspiring to join in.

Right: Here leather is interpreted in a different way. Janet Halligan achieves this fascinating effect by using stoneware glazes on the surface of her hand-built trompe l'oeil objects.

Above: This luster-decorated bowl, by Jonathan Chiswell Jones, shows a circular "canvas," divided geometrically to give an effect that is formal and considered—the decoration fitting perfectly into the space allowed.

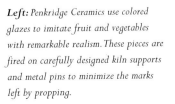

Right: A simple band of texture around this early 20th-century cooking pot accentuates the high shoulder of an essentially classical form.

Left: Penkridge Ceramics use colored glazes to imitate fruit and vegetables with remarkable realism. These pieces are fired on carefully designed kiln supports and metal pins to minimize the marks left by propping.

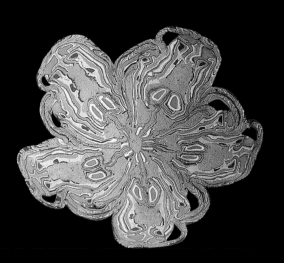
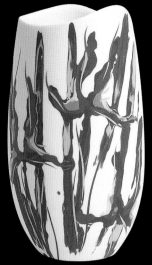

Chapter 1 TECHNIQUES USED DURING THE MAKING PROCESS

A marriage between form and decoration is the goal of most potters. Working directly into or onto the raw clay gives the best possible chance of a harmonious result. From impressing into clay to printing onto it, the techniques described in this chapter give enormous scope for combining form and surface with little or no need for intervention at later stages.

ADDITIONS AT THE RAW CLAY STAGE

COMBUSTIBLE AND INCOMBUSTIBLE MATERIALS can be mixed or pressed into clay before or during the making process. The final effect on the surface will depend on the reaction the material has when it is fired. Combustible materials burn away, while incombustible ones tend to meld into the clay.

Above: *Some of the combustible materials that can be mixed into clay (clockwise from top left): paper pulp (bought or homemade), sawdust, lentils, couscous grains, rice, and paper.*

COMBUSTIBLE MATERIALS

Adding combustible materials to clay is not a new idea—even the Bible records the use of straw and clay for making bricks. It may seem odd to add a material that burns away during firing, but there are sound reasons for it. The addition of straw, paper, or fibers "opens up" the clay, so that it dries more evenly. The resulting material is less prone to cracking and warping and has a greater strength. Bricks made from adobe (clay and straw) are surprisingly strong even when unfired.

SURFACE QUALITIES

In this book, however, we are especially concerned with the surface qualities produced by such additions. When material burns out of clay it usually disappears completely—or leaves just a trace of whitish ash. We are therefore left with a textured and probably pitted surface over which color can be applied. This will fall into the indentations, accentuating subtle but distinctive textures. Harder objects can also be rolled and pressed into clay and left to burn away, using the appropriate making processes.

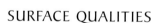

Top: This form was built with paper clay slabs and coated with copper slip. Tapioca grains were pressed into the surface, then coated with porcelain slip. After biscuit firing, a barium glaze was applied and washed off, so that it remained in the round holes made by the tapioca. Final firing was at 2228°F (1220°C). RUTH LYNE
Center: Form and texture combine to striking effect in these forms made from paper clay, copper oxide, and contrasting earthenware glazes. FRANK SMITH
Bottom: Surface effect produced with porcelain slip and wooden cocktail sticks. ANNE BRODIE

HEALTH AND SAFETY

There will be considerable fumes during firing as the materials combust. Good ventilation is essential and outdoor firing preferable.

COMBUSTIBLE ADDITIONS

- Paper pulp/cotton linter (typically 10–30% paper to clay)
- Seeds, lentils, beans, rice, etc.
- Polystyrene beads
- Fabric, string
- Sawdust
- Plant material

INCOMBUSTIBLE ADDITIONS

- Nails, staples, metal mesh, metal filings
- Glass—from a supplier, or recycled bottles
- Fired clay, crushed as grog, in various grades
- Stone chippings

INCOMBUSTIBLE MATERIALS

Added materials that remain after firing can also produce interesting surfaces, whether mixed into the clay or pressed into its surface. Some materials are partially destroyed and leave traces—metals, for example, withstand varying temperatures. Other inclusions, such as glass, melt and distort to become part of the fired ceramic. This presents an entirely different way of working. The fired surface can be glazed, if you wish, but can be considered finished when you decide it is! Beginning with a stained clay is also a possibility.

DIFFERENT APPROACHES

Additions of this nature affect the working properties of the clay, usually making it more difficult to use. Obviously if glass or metal is added, the clay cannot be safely handled, and alternative methods must be found—casting into molds, for example. Some potters spend much time polishing the hard, fired surface with an angle grinder and diamond pads to achieve a kind of "terrazzo" effect (see David Binns' work on page 17).

METAL, GLASS, AND "GROG"

Items such as steel nails, staples, and safety pins can become a feature of the piece. These can be fired to at least 1940°F (1060°C) before they disintegrate. Copper or brass melt at lower temperatures. Crushed glass put into grooves or hollows in the clay forms luscious, glossy pools when fired. The optimum temperature for firing depends upon the glass. Use broken bottles, or buy more refined crushed glass from the manufacturers, in fine or coarse grades. Refined glass will probably require firing at a lower temperature, around 1832°F (1000°C), or colors may fade.

Fired clay, known as "grog," is often added to clay bodies. It changes the working properties and introduces texture of a fine or coarse nature, depending on the grade. There is also white grog, known as molochite.

BASIC TOOLBOX

Materials to add to clay

Knife and other basic hand tools

Rolling pin

Canvas

Above: *Some of the incombustible materials that can be mixed into clay (clockwise from top left): fine white grog (molochite), tacks, iron spangles, crushed blue glass, finely powdered red glass, fiber-glass chopped strands, coarse buff grog, brass turnings (in center).*

Above: *A hand-built pitcher made using clay and nails has an organic shape and texture that was accentuated by raku firing.* JOHN COMMANE

USING INCOMBUSTIBLE MATERIALS

1 Cut a slab of clay to shape and allow it to stiffen a little before folding it so that the edges touch. Stand upright and ease into shape.

2 Press the edges carefully together—a little slip on the join can help here. Secure with tacks—these become partly functional and partly decorative.

↑ The piece was raku fired after coating with a copper glaze that adds to the metallic effect (*see also page 124*).

15

ADDITIONS AT THE RAW CLAY STAGE

CHAPTER 1

Combustible Materials

PAPER CLAY HAS BECOME increasingly popular as potters discover the wonderful versatility of this material. The addition of paper pulp changes the working properties of clay dramatically. Cellulose fibrous tubes in the paper increase flexibility and help to knit the clay together as it dries. Paper clay can be used in very thin sheets, and offers amazing freedom in the building of sculptural work. Its adaptability solves many of the constructional problems presented by regular clay.

YOU WILL NEED

Newspaper / paper pulp

Pressure cooker (optional)

Glaze mixer

Bucket

Slip

Two lengths of wood approx. 2 ft (60cm) long

Plaster slab for drying clay

Knife

Ruler or straight edge

1 Tear newspaper along the grain to make strips. Add the strips to water and pressure cook to soften. (Cooking will speed up the process but it is not essential.) Place the softened paper in a bucket with enough water to allow a glaze mixer to reduce it to pulp.

2 Add slip to the paper pulp and mix again. The ratio of slip to paper is normally 10–30% by volume, but this is a matter of choice. Any clay can be used to make the slip. Allow the mixture to stand for a few days to settle, and pour off the surface water.

3 Mix the slurry again and pour it onto a dry plaster slab. Level the edges, using two slats of wood. As water is absorbed by the plaster, the mixture shrinks in volume and becomes a thinner, more compacted slab. Leave for approximately an hour to dry.

4 Run a knife along the slats, and peel the clay away from the plaster, ready for use. The clay is flexible and the surface has the mealy texture typical of paper clay.

VARIATIONS

Left: *Poppy seeds were added to the slip coating on this ceramic panel to achieve the textured effect.* RUTH LYNE
Center: *String, coated with slip and applied to the surface, created this texture of ripples and eddies. Both these panels have oxide washes and dry glazes and were fired to 2228°F (1220°C).* RUTH LYNE
Right: *Detail of coil-built vessel. Polystyrene beads were pressed into the clay while it was still wet and burned away leaving holes.* SARAH LEYMAN

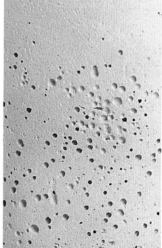

Incombustible Materials

THIS DEMONSTRATION ILLUSTRATES A very personal way of combining metal with clay. Chicken wire mesh is formed into a vessel shape and used as an armature to be covered with clay. During firing the mesh, clay, and glaze melt together to become one. It is a technique that can be adapted to make various shapes and is particularly suited to complicated sculptural forms.

YOU WILL NEED

Chicken wire 2 x 2 ft (60 x 60cm)

Wire cutters

Cheesecloth 2 x 2 ft (60 x 60cm)

String

Paper-clay slurry

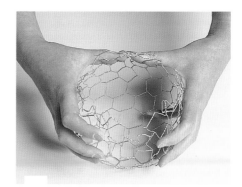

1 Cut a piece of wire mesh with wire cutters and form it by hand into the required shape.

COMBINING METAL AND CLAY

2 Once you are happy with the shape of the armature, wrap it in cheesecloth and bind the edges with string to secure.

3 Brush a thick coat of paper-clay slurry over the surface. It will stick to the cheesecloth. Allow to dry before biscuit firing.

HEALTH AND SAFETY

Beware damage to the kiln shelves, because substances can melt and spoil them. Use an old shelf until you are sure of what is going to happen in the kiln. Take care when handling shelves and pots, which may have sharp protrusions. Do not allow "contaminated" clay to enter general circulation.

← When fired, the mesh integrates with the clay, and the cheesecloth and string burn away. The biscuit-fired form can be glazed or colored in any way, but low-temperature firing is recommended. This piece, by Ruth Lyne, was raku fired to approximately 1832°F (1000°C) with a copper glaze.

VARIATIONS

Below: Brass lathe turnings are pressed into the clay and fired to 1832°F (1000°C). The result is a heavy black metallic finish due to overloading with copper oxide.

Center: Crushed glass of different grades is rolled into the surface. The piece was fired to 1832°F (1000°C).

Right: Curved standing form in porcelain with a pebble aggregate, which was fired to 2156°F (1180°C), then diamond ground. DAVID BINNS

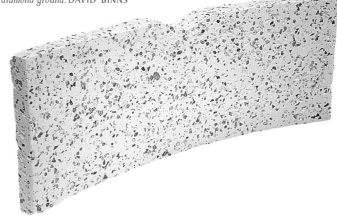

THE ADDITION OF COLOR TO CLAY

CLAY IS FOUND in many geographical locations and in a variety of colors. The color mainly depends upon the influence of metallic oxides during its formation and the amount of carbonaceous material that it contains. Although the clay's appearance gives some indication of its fired color, it can often be misleading. For example, an ocher-colored clay can fire plant-pot red, and a dark gray clay can come out ivory.

Clays sold by pottery suppliers are labeled so that you know what color to expect. They include black clays that fire the color of dark chocolate. Compare this with the marble white of porcelain, and you will see what a vast array there is to choose from. Mixing and marbling them is a wonderful way to create pattern, but beware—clays have different shrinkage rates and can split apart as they dry or are fired. There are scientific methods for ascertaining the compatibility of clays, but experimentation is the most straightforward way. As a general rule, choose clays with similar firing temperatures and similar textures. However, daring combinations can bring unexpected rewards, and are worth trying.

The simplest way to begin practicing with colored clays is to use two bought clays of contrasting color that fire happily together. You can buy ready-mixed colored clays, but they are expensive—and mixing your own is not difficult.

Top: Slab-built porcelain vases decorated using inlays of colored clays and slips. SUSAN NEMETH
Center: *Press-molded bowl in porcelain with body inlaid slip decoration.* SUSAN NEMETH
Bottom: *Earthenware plate, colored clays rolled into the surface and formed by the jigger and jolley method.* SABINA TEUTEBERG

HEALTH AND SAFETY

- Take sensible precautions when using colored clays—wash hands regularly, and wear a mask when weighing and mixing the stains.
- If you have sensitive or broken skin, wear surgical gloves when handling colors and clays.

MAKING COLORED CLAY

Use a white or very pale clay with the working properties you need. For example, a textured clay is easier for hand-building, and a smooth clay can be preferable for throwing.

YOU WILL NEED

Scales
White clay
Mortar or rolling pin
*Body / slip stain,
 underglaze color,
 or oxides
 (see recipes opposite)*
Bowl
80s mesh sieve
Canvas

1 Dry the clay, rolling it into thin slabs to speed the process. Grind the dry clay into coarse crumbs in a mortar, or between two sheets of plastic. Weigh approximately 28 oz (800g) of dry clay and place it in a container.

2 Weigh out the stain according to your recipe for coloring 2.2 lb (1kg) of clay, and mix the stain with a little water in a jug.

ALTERNATIVE METHOD FOR COLORING CLAY

Begin by mixing a blue stain into porcelain—approximately 0.35 oz (10g) of color to 2.2 lb (1kg) of clay will give a vibrant blue. (This is an alternative method from the one described on the previous page.)

YOU WILL NEED

2.2 lb (1kg) clay
0.35 oz (10g) blue stain
Plaster slab
Paintbrush

3 Sieve it into the dry clay and add more water to cover the mixture. Allow to stand for about 30 minutes and then stir to make a thick slip. If too thin, allow it to stand until some surface water can be poured off.

1 Roll out several small rounds of clay into slabs of roughly even thickness. Mix the color as in the previous method, then add water to make a soft paste. Brush the color onto the first piece of clay.

2 Sandwich the colored paste and clay in layers until it is all used up. Compact it firmly together and begin kneading.

3 Knead until a uniform color is obtained. It may help to knead on a plaster slab, or to leave the mixture to dry a little first. This is a messy process and you may prefer to wear rubber gloves.

4 Pour the thick slip or slurry onto a plaster slab and allow to dry until it peels from the slab. Knead it, and seal it in a labeled bag ready for later use. You will now have approximately 2.2 lb (1kg) of plastic clay.

RECIPES FOR COLORED CLAYS

The recipes below give some indication of the colors achievable with a limited number of pigments. The amounts shown are for 2.2 lb (1kg) of white clay. The colors and oxides can be used as they are, or in the combinations listed. Most stains need 0.35–1 oz (10–30g), depending on the color strength required. An enormous color palette can be achieved with a little experimentation.

Body stains: Canary yellow, orange, pink, sky or bright blue, black
Oxides: Cobalt, copper, red iron, manganese

COLOR	STAIN OR OXIDE	QUANTITY
Blue	Cobalt Oxide A little Red Iron can dull the color, or Copper can add a green tinge	0.03–0.35 oz (1–10g) (max)
Turquoise	Sky Blue Canary Yellow	0.35 oz (10g) 0.7 oz (20g)
Bright Green	Sky Blue Canary Yellow	0.7 oz (20g) 1 oz (30g)
Light Olive Green	Egg Yellow Stain Cobalt Oxide	0.35 oz (10g) 0.07 oz (2g)
Dark Olive Green	Egg Yellow Stain Cobalt Oxide	0.35 oz (10g) 0.14 oz (4g)
Mustard	Orange Stain Red Iron Oxide	0.7 oz (20g) 0.3 oz (8g)
Light Purple	Pink Stain Cobalt Oxide	0.9 oz (25g) 0.07 oz (2g)
Dark Purple	Pink Stain Cobalt Oxide	0.9 oz (25g) 0.14 oz (4g)
Khaki or Green	Copper Oxide gives khaki without glaze; green with glaze	0.35 oz–0.9 oz (10–25g)
Black (A)	Black Body Stain	1.5 oz (45g)
Black (B)	Cobalt Oxide Copper Carbonate Manganese Dioxide	0.5 oz (15g) 0.5 oz (15g) 0.5 oz (15g)

Below: Samples showing a white clay colored with different oxides and body stains, which have then been stoneware fired with no glaze.

Thrown Agate

WHEN CLAY IS THROWN ON the wheel the particles become aligned in a spiral formation. This is illustrated to perfection by throwing with a mixture of colored clays.

Begin by mixing a blue stain into porcelain, as described on pages 18–19. A wide color palette can be used, but here we are throwing with just blue and white, which shows a striking contrast.

YOU WILL NEED

White porcelain clay
Blue porcelain clay
Wheel
Loop-ended tool
Metal kidney

1 To prepare a block of porcelain for throwing agate, make a sandwich of white and blue clays, with the blue clay in the middle. Take care to avoid air pockets, and be sure that the blue and white clays are of the same consistency.

2 Center the clay on the wheel.

Before opening it up, remove a core from the **3** middle with a loop tool. This stops the bowl from becoming lined with white clay.

VARIATIONS

Left: *Soda-glazed porcelain cup and saucer. Different colored clays are expertly arranged on the wheel in such a way as to create intriguing patterns on the surface.* JACK DOHERTY

Center left: *Conical porcelain vessel made using the process shown above.* BRIDGET ALDRIDGE

Center right: *Unglazed porcelain vase. This illustrates the subtlety of color that can be achieved by throwing stained clays. The colors appear in different densities according to the way they have been arranged during the throwing process.* REG MOON

Far right: *Bottle, thrown with terra cotta and porcelain clays. The surface was carefully refined by turning and polishing before firing to 2282°F (1250°C). Unglazed.* LES RUCINSKI

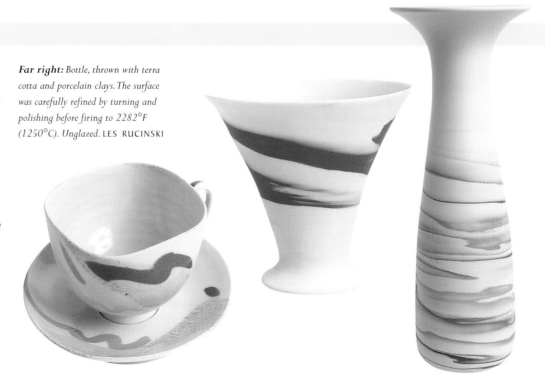

4 Throw the bowl as directly as possible, using only a few "pulls." This keeps the stripe bold.

5 At this stage the bowl is kept quite thick and with a substantial base, which will be turned later into a deep foot ring. This will give the bowl "lift," adding to its elegance and lightness.

6 The effect may look blurred, but now allow the form to dry sufficiently to be turned. Upon turning, the stripe will emerge crisp and sharp. A metal kidney can help to scrape the surface of the form.

When biscuit fired (*left*), the blue is pale and the porcelain fairly soft. The surface can be refined with emery paper before firing again to a higher temperature, when both clay and color become much stronger (*right*). This example, by Bridget Aldridge, was gas fired to 2300°F (1260°C) in a reduction atmosphere to achieve translucency and depth of color, and is not glazed.

Hand-built Agate

THIS IS A METHOD of rolling clays to give a strata effect. There are many different ways of hand building with colored clays. Clays can be coiled, rolled, stacked, sliced, and rearranged to give a whole range of effects. The illustrations below show just one method that makes use of rolling and stretching colored clays to give a particular effect reminiscent of rock strata. The clays are manipulated in such a way as to stretch into subtly layered stripes, and fault lines are introduced by cutting or tearing. The thin sheet of clay is laminated onto a backing slab so that it can be used to build with.

YOU WILL NEED
Different colored clays
Rolling pin
Canvas to roll on
Knife
Plaster molds, if 3-D
  forms are to be made

1 Roll a variety of thin and fat coils from batches of differently colored clays. Twist the coils together—the tighter the twist, the finer the stripes will be.

2 Flatten the coils with a rolling pin to form a thin striped slab. Only roll in one direction at this stage to keep the width of the different colored lines even.

3 Cut the slab and rearrange the halves to introduce a fault line in the pattern. Roll the pieces again so that they become joined together.

4 Place the rejoined halves on a slab of the same clay, and roll again to laminate them to the backing slab. Continue rolling to achieve the required effect. Eventually the colors stretch and some become almost translucent, revealing other colors beneath.

← The finished piece by Jo Connell: a double-walled, leaf-shaped bowl, 18 in (45cm) long, in unglazed stoneware. This hollow form was press-molded in two halves and joined at the leatherhard stage.

VARIATIONS

Right: *These pieces show different combinations of colors and patterns put together in the same way as illustrated above. The center one is salt-glazed, using terra cotta and porcelain clays as well as cobalt and iron stains. The other two pieces are unglazed stoneware, given an electric firing at 2282°F (1250°C).*

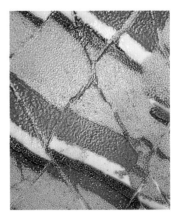

Colored Clay Appliqué

YOU WILL NEED

Different colored clays
Rolling pin
Knife
Canvas to roll on
Plaster molds if 3-D forms
are to be made

THE SAME PRINCIPLES AS shown on the previous page are used again here. Clay pieces are rolled out thinly, placed onto a backing slab and rolled again. In this case a defined leaf shape is cut out and applied to the surface. It could be attached with a little water or slip and left raised, but here it is rolled into the backing slab so that the whole surface becomes flush and on one level.

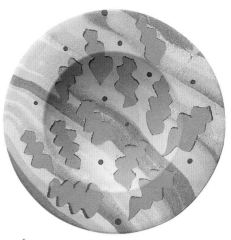

↑ Oak leaf bowl by Jo Connell, press-molded in two parts and joined to make a hollow form. 10 in (25cm) diameter.

1 Roll out and stack two thin slabs. Roll gently but firmly to bond the slabs, and use an angled cut to create a leaf shape whose outline reveals the underneath color.

2 Position the leaf shape onto a ready rolled backing slab, which must be of a similar soft consistency for the two pieces to join smoothly when rolled.

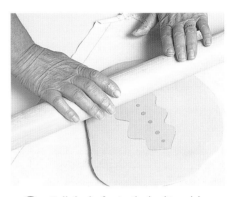

3 Roll the leaf onto the backing slab, and a "shadow" will emerge around its edges as both layers of clay stretch. Dots applied down the center of the leaf add extra detail and these too will begin to merge.

ALTERNATIVE METHOD: COLORED CLAY SLICES

1 Stack thin slabs of different colored clay. Roll them up tightly to eliminate air. Slice them into similar pieces of even thickness.

2 Roll into one sheet of clay. If the surface smudges it can be rectified by careful scraping at the late leatherhard stage, or by sanding after biscuit firing.

VARIATIONS

Left: *Agate-ware bowl. Colored clay was rolled and folded, then chopped into pieces and assembled on a flat surface. It was then rolled until joined completely and the slab was pressed into a plaster mold. When dry it was rubbed with wire wool to reveal a crisper surface and fired to 2300°F (1260°C).* MAL MAGSON
Center and right: *Details of two press-molded plates. Tiny rolls of pale-colored clays were placed on a colored background and then rolled into the*

surface. Cobalt oxide was used to stain the background on the left, copper oxide was used on the right. JO CONNELL

23

TEXTURES

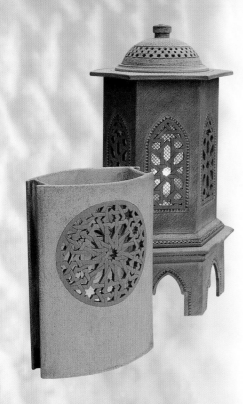

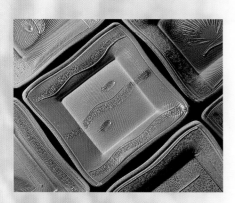

When a child is handed a lump of clay, his or her first reaction is almost always the same—to push a finger into it and to start making marks. There could scarcely be a material more receptive to surface texturing than clay. It is soft and malleable, gives under the slightest pressure, yet retains any imprint imposed upon it. The effect can be dried and fired for posterity. Textured surfaces are satisfying to the eye; the play of light and shade shows ever-varied aspects of the piece. Texture is also pleasing to the touch, and this is one of the most intriguing features of ceramics. It is hard to resist the tactile quality of clay.

This section deals with techniques for creating effects on or in the clay surface itself. There are many ways to achieve textures at different stages in the making process, but when clay is in its soft, plastic state it is particularly inviting. A flat slab of clay is easy to handle, and once textured can be used in many ways: as a tile or plaque in its own right; as a slab with which to construct, or to press-mold into a bowl; or for more complex forms.

BASIC TOOLBOX

Suitable clay

Canvas

Rolling pin

Craft knives

Modeling tools

Objects for producing texture such as natural forms, mechanical objects

Modeling clay and plaster (for roulettes and stamps)

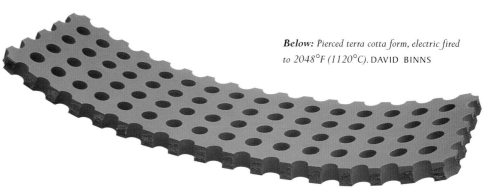

Below: *Pierced terra cotta form, electric fired to 2048°F (1120°C).* DAVID BINNS

Below: *A wide range of tools is used to add texture to clay. From left to right: potter's knife; sgraffito tool; strip-turning tools; coil-maker tool; tapered hole cutter; steel tool (for carving); hardwood modeling tools.*

Top: *Lamp and lantern built from slabs, apart from the lantern lid, which was coiled. Pierced and colored with high-firing body stains in slip. Fired to 2273°F (1245°C).* NIGEL EDMONDSON

Center: *Porcelain bowl thrown in sections and slumped. Textured using porcelain slip, manipulated using rubber kidney and fingers. Fired to 2408°F (1320°C).* JOANNA HOWELLS

Bottom: *Soda-glazed bowls using colored slips and impressed decoration.* MAY LING BEADSMOORE

It is important to remember that the clay surface, while easily textured, can be just as easily damaged, and the potter must seek to retain the crispness of the impressions created. This can be difficult when constructing with textured pieces, and great care is necessary. Planning is the key. Decide exactly what you want to make, and your pot will stand a better chance of emerging with a fresh, spontaneous surface instead of the signs of false starts, indecision, and accidental fingerprints!

The textures illustrated vary from an almost "distressed" surface—created by impressing an organic object, such as a rock or fossil—to the controlled and accurate use of a sharp craft knife for incising and piercing. Texture can be heavy or subtle, organized or random. The choice of glaze or color is important in making the most of this altered surface. A light spray of color can be a good way to bring out the subtleties of a textured surface, whereas a thick, opaque glaze can obscure it altogether. A shiny, translucent glaze can also be useful in accentuating texture, because the color will appear more intense where it is thicker.

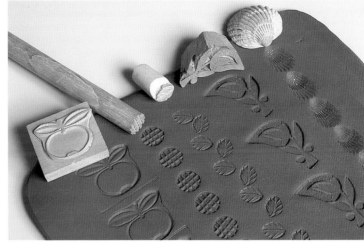

Above: A stamped clay slab showing the tools used. Left to right: rubber stamp; carved wooden doweling; biscuit-fired stamp; wooden print block, and a shell.

Below: Double-slabbed bowl. One thin slab impressed with foliage, seed pods and cones, is laid on top and press-molded into a thicker base slab. ANDREW MASON

Below: Hand-built "Celtic Ewe" in white stoneware. Slabs of clay are impressed and stamped with a range of natural and man-made objects, torn and stretched, then rejoined in different patterns and orders. A matte white glaze is used thickly and thinly, fired to 2048°F (1120°C) (oxidized). JAN BEENY

25

Left: Textured stoneware vessel with dry glaze. CARLOS VAN REISBURG VERSLUYS

TEXTURES

CHAPTER 1

Impressing

SOFT CLAY TAKES AN IMPRESSION very easily, so this is an ideal way to start experimenting with textural decoration. Objects can be pushed into clay to give many different effects. The harder the clay becomes, the less deep the impression will be. An interesting way to work with impressing is to apply texture to slabs of soft clay and construct with them as they stiffen up. The slabs can be formed by simple press-molding or wrapping around a form, as well as by conventional slab-building methods.

YOU WILL NEED

Soft clay

Rolling pin

Objects to create impressions, such as cork, wood, leaves, or other found objects

1 Objects pressed into a clay surface create an attractive reverse print. Rocks and fossils make interesting marks, and so do many other natural forms, such as cork, wood, bark, coral, and shell. This technique is similar to stamping (page 32), but using found objects instead of manufactured stamps.

2 A rolling pin is useful for pressing a delicate object into clay, but do not roll too many times in different directions or a blurred print can result. Some objects, such as feathers or soft plant material, give an extremely subtle print, which can be lost if glazed. Careful coloring can accentuate such fine detail.

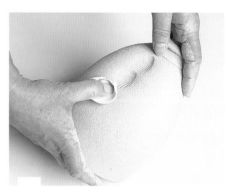

3 At the opposite extreme is a holey rubber mat, which makes a bold print in the clay. This was achieved by placing the mat on the floor and throwing a clay slab down onto it. Throwing the clay in this way ensures maximum contact and gives a deep, even impression.

4 Working into a three-dimensional form adds another degree of difficulty—the process is harder to control, and pressing too hard can cause collapse. Support the work from the inside with fingers or tools against which to push.

VARIATIONS

Top, left to right: *Ferns, netting, or a rubber car mat can be used to create interesting textures in clay.*

Bottom left: *Shell impressions are used decoratively on these thrown, soda-fired, stoneware beakers.*
MAY LING BEADSMOORE

Bottom right: *Molochite grogged stoneware was impressed with coniferous foliage, seedpods and cones, then press-molded into a thicker base slab. Glaze was brushed and sprayed on, and then the piece was fired to 2192°F (1200°C) several times.* ANDREW MASON

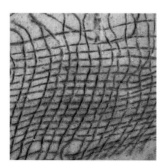

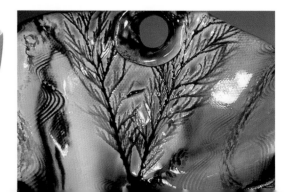

Piercing

Piercing means cutting completely through the clay to make a hole, and extreme care is needed to avoid weakening the pot.

The demonstration makes piercing look simple, but the technique calls for skill developed through practice, a steady hand, and an excellent eye for pattern and symmetry—both positive and negative.

The clay used here is porcelain, a beautifully smooth body with which to work, allowing the sharp, thin-bladed knife to move freely. It is also fragile at this leatherhard stage and must be kept damp enough to avoid becoming brittle—though not so soft that it will distort when handled. An even consistency throughout the piece is essential.

This bowl was wheel thrown, but many making processes lend themselves to pierced decoration.

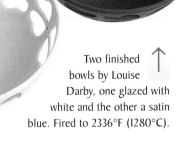

Two finished bowls by Louise Darby, one glazed with white and the other a satin blue. Fired to 2336°F (1280°C).

1 Center the pot on a banding wheel, and draw penciled guidelines on it for spacing. Drill the central holes, and begin the process of piercing.

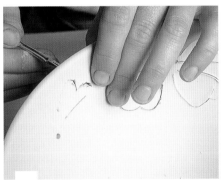

2 Working quickly to prevent the clay from becoming brittle (and possibly cracking), roughly cut out the entire design and then refine it.

3 When piercing is complete, lightly sponge the cut edges to remove burrs, and leave the pot to dry slowly. The work is very fragile at this stage, and if moved, it must be cupped in two hands and picked up from the base.

27

VARIATIONS

Left: *Table lamp hand-built from slabs, then pierced and colored using high-firing body stains in slip.*
NIGEL EDMONDSON

Right: *Two porcelain vases pierced and inlaid with black glaze, which is also used on the insides.* LOUISE DARBY

Rouletting

YOU WILL NEED

Modeling clay

Relief-textured object

Former—such as a broom handle or similar

Adhesive tape

ROULETTING USES A RANGE of tools that are rolled across the clay surface to make textures. You can buy roulettes from pottery suppliers, improvise them from machine parts, or make your own from scratch.

This sequence shows a personal approach to rouletting. If you make your own roulettes, source material can be derived from everyday objects such as textured plastic, leaves, metal mesh, and woodgrain.

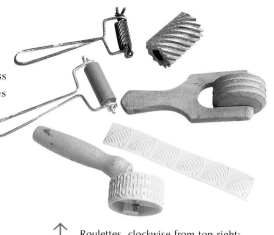

↑ Roulettes, clockwise from top right: Old machine part; antique kitchen implement; purpose-made roulette with detachable plastic belts; small print roller; improvised roulettes using wire handles from print rollers to hold small machine parts.

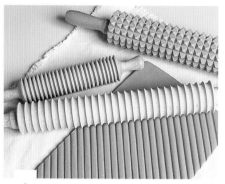

↑ Roulettes are like mini rolling pins, and these textured rolling pins (intended for the kitchen) are excellent tools for use on a flat clay surface. Rollers can also be made from plaster: pour the plaster into a cardboard tube, peel off the cardboard when the plaster is set, and carve away.

1 Roll out a piece of modeling clay and press it firmly onto an original relief texture. Here, a plaster tile is used, but this could be a three-dimensional object, since the modeling clay is sufficiently flexible to wrap around a form without damaging it. Also pictured is a reverse plaster print that was cast from the same plaster tile.

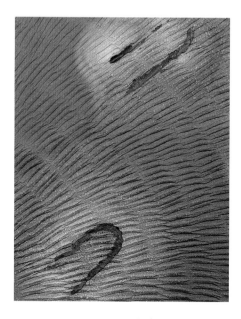

2 Wrap the modeling clay print around a suitable former, and secure it firmly with adhesive tape.

VARIATIONS

Left: *Wood-fired terra cotta tripod vessel with roulette decoration.*
JONATHAN GARRATT

Center left: *Galvanized staples were set on a wood-fired terra cotta disk that had been textured with a roulette tool.*
JONATHAN GARRATT

Center right: *On this piece entitled "Beach Huts in Dunes," a ridged rolling pin was used to create texture, which was then accentuated by salt glazing.*
JO CONNELL

Right: *Wood-fired terra cotta decorative piece, with white slip over roulette decoration, fired to 2066°F (1130°C).* JONATHAN GARRATT

Far right: *Pattern made with the roulette shown above. The color comes*

from copper oxide under a dry barium glaze, fired to 2282°F (1250°C).
JO CONNELL

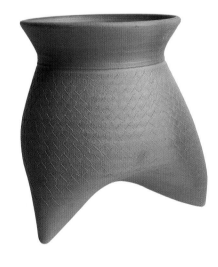

3 Seal the tube of clay at the base with another plug of modeling clay, then stand it upright and fill it with plaster.

4 Allow it to set for about 10 minutes and remove the modeling clay. When the plaster roulette is fully dry, it can be used in a number of ways.

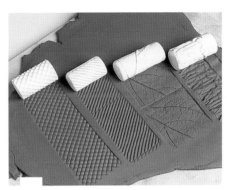

5 Impressions made by these roulettes on a flat surface give some indication of the variety of effects you can achieve.

6 Rouletting on the wheel. One hand supports the pot from inside, while the other rotates the plaster roulette.

← The finished piece by Les Rucinski. A wash of white terra sigillata (*see page 72*) was applied after biscuit firing and wiped back to accentuate the texture. Fired to 2048°F (1120°C).

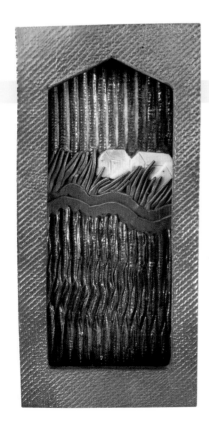

Incising

INCISING SIMPLY MEANS cutting into the clay surface, and involves a wide range of approaches. The incisions can be subtle or bold and can be introduced at various stages of the making process.

Incised lines can be made in clay at any stage until it is biscuit fired—and even then some clays are soft enough to carve. Remember that a soft, textured clay will take less precise lines than a harder, smoother one. It may be necessary to refine the surface with emery paper after biscuit firing. Lines can be emphasized by the use of glaze, or with oxides and pigments (*see page 96*).

The lines created in this example reflect a distinctive drawing style and show skilled and fluid use of tools.

YOU WILL NEED

Leatherhard piece to decorate

Hacksaw blade

Sponge

Pencil

Craft knife or excise knife and a variety of blades

Metal kidney

1 Draw freehand onto the leatherhard clay in pencil. It is useful to have a sketchbook of drawings for reference. Note that this stoneware body has a fairly smooth texture.

2 Once the design is drawn, incising begins. In this case an adapted hacksaw blade is used. Incising needs to be done boldly to achieve fluid lines. Remove small burrs of clay with a sponge.

3 Continue to build up the outlines of the design, cleaning up the surface as the work progresses and removing excess clay produced by the incising process.

4 Larger areas of clay are removed with an excise knife—changing the blades gives different thicknesses and depths of line.

VARIATIONS

Below and right: *The pitcher was made by the method shown above. The "badger" pebbles were formed from a more textured clay, and the incisions and texture were accentuated by the contrasting glaze.* LOUISE DARBY
Center: *Detail of salt-glazed vessel with incised decoration and colored slips.* JO CONNELL

Right: *Coil-built form with incised Celtic knot decoration.* FRANK SMITH
Far right: *Lifesize torso incised with images of water and mythical scenes.* ANDREW COX

5 A combination of narrow and broad areas of clay are removed as the design takes shape. The clay is cut deeply enough to fill with glaze at a later stage.

6 Once all the incising has been completed the piece is biscuit fired and then dipped in glaze. It is now allowed to become "touch dry," but not powdery.

7 Glaze is scraped away from the surface with a metal kidney but remains in the indentations of the incised design.

 The finished frog bowl, by Louise Darby, was fired to 2336°F (1280°C) in a light reduction atmosphere. The decoration on this piece is thoughtfully applied—the inside, outside, and the footring all seen as being equally important. The bowl is displayed on a mirror to show the intricate decoration on all surfaces. Detail shown below.

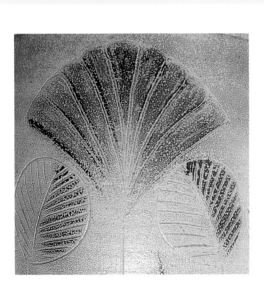

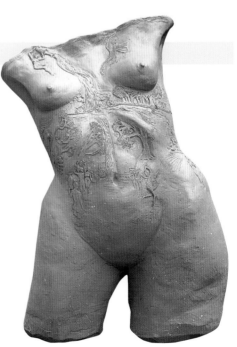

Stamping

A STAMP IS AN object that is pushed into clay to make a print. Stamps can be natural or manufactured and they are usually small—they need to be a convenient shape and size to be held firmly, yet small enough to leave impressions on a slightly curved surface. Shells make good stamps, and so do old lead or wooden printblocks— or you can create your own stamps. Here are just two of the many methods that can be used to make stamps.

YOU WILL NEED

Leatherhard clay
Incising tool
Small cardboard tubes
Smooth board
Latex
Slip trailer
Plaster
Modeling clay
Slip

↑ A finished piece by Paul Young that shows stamped decoration with colored earthenware glazes.

METHOD 1 • CARVED STAMPS

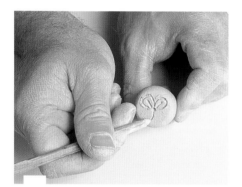

1 Biscuit-fired clay is good for stamping; because it is porous, it is less likely to stick to the clay. A stamp can be carved out of leatherhard clay and biscuit fired at 1832°F (1000°C). A variety of tools can be used for carving a design on the stamp. In this case a sharp pencil has been chosen.

2 All these stamps are made from clay, carved, and biscuit fired. Another good material for making stamps is plaster. To make stamps from plaster, pour plaster into a small cardboard tube or box and, when set, remove the cardboard and carve into the end face in the same way as step 1. Allow to dry before use (*see* Rouletting, *pages 28–29*).

3 Small pads of clay were applied to this pitcher and then stamped. Stamping ensures that the pads of clay bond well to the surface of the jug. If the jug is too dry, a little slip will help the stamped pad of clay to stick. A hand should be placed inside the jug to make sure that the walls do not distort with the pressure of stamping.

VARIATIONS

Left: *Slab-built box in high-fired red clay, unglazed. The surface is created by texturing with wire wool and stamping to give a stitched effect.* LES RUCINSKI
Center: *Salt-glazed jug with stamping detail.* JIM MALONE
Right: *Detail of stamping decoration on salt-glazed dish, with slips beneath.* ROSEMARY COCHRANE

METHOD 2 • MOLDED STAMPS

1 Here, a stamp is made not by carving but by making a small plaster mold of a raised pattern created by latex. The latex is trailed onto a board in the desired pattern. It should not be too large—a small stamp tends to give a more precise imprint.

2 A retaining wall is built around the pattern with clay, and the plaster is poured in. For further tips on the use of plaster, see Molds, page 36.

3 Once the plaster is dry, carefully pull away the clay that was used for the retaining wall and lift the block of plaster up from the board.

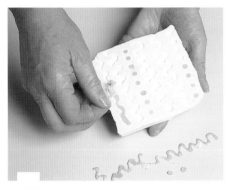

4 The latex is removed from the plaster and the mold tidied up before being left to dry completely.

5 The mold now becomes a stamp, which can be pressed into clay. The aim here was to simulate the stitching and patterns found in patchwork quilts.

↑ The finished piece: a patchwork-quilt plate by Christine Geddes. White earthenware clay, stamped, and transparent earthenware glaze applied.

33

ALTERNATIVE STAMP

A stamp carved from clay and then biscuit fired is used to press into the base of this thrown and slabbed dish while it is still soft.

↑ Finished piece by Rosemary Cochrane. Press-molded "fish" handles were added and the texture accentuated by salt-glazing (see pages 104–105).

Marks Made on the Wheel

ONE OF THE MOST direct ways of decorating is to include the decoration in the making process. The making marks are interesting in themselves and uniquely harmonious with the form of the piece.

Throwing on the wheel is an excellent example of a process in which making and decorating come together. "Throwing rings" that occur naturally can be used as a feature in their own right. Whereas in other methods of decoration the rings can be a hindrance, here they echo the spiral nature of the throwing process and celebrate the plastic qualities of clay.

The finished piece: a free-thrown bowl by John Commane in reduced stoneware, 8 in (20cm) in diameter. →

YOU WILL NEED

Potter's wheel

Clay

Tools for marking such as bamboo modeling tool, wooden rib, plastic fork, wide-toothed comb

↑ Thrown thinly to the point of distortion, this piece makes use of throwing rings both inside and out. Take care not to collapse or tear the clay, and leave extra depth at the base of the pot for the start of the spiral groove, and for a footring, if required. The wheel should be turning slowly, and the pot is thinned gradually from base to rim. Allow the pot to stiffen slightly before removing from the wheel or continuing work on it.

ALTERNATIVE TOOLS

A freshly thrown flat plate is marked with a serrated plastic kitchen tool. Wide, fairly shallow markings are produced.

The same form, marked with a wooden "rib." The artist applies a calculated amount of pressure evenly throughout the process.

The thumb digs into the plate and moves the clay into a spiral. This is a simple method but it requires a steady hand and concentration.

VARIATIONS

Left: *Flat-based bowl marked with a bamboo modeling tool after construction was complete.* JO CONNELL

Center: *Thrown pot with ridge marks that were made around the base during the throwing process.* STEVE TAYLOR

Right: *A detail of marks made during the throwing of a bowl—the only tools used being the potter's fingers.* JOHN COMMANE

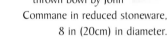

Burnishing

YOU WILL NEED

Leatherhard clay

*Spoon or smooth
  stone/bone/wooden
  modeling tool*

Vegetable oil (optional)

Beeswax

BURNISHING COMPRESSES the clay particles in a polishing action and it can help to make the clay less porous. It is simple and effective, but it is a time-consuming process. A smooth clay is easier to burnish than a textured one but applying a coating of slip over a textured clay body will provide a smooth surface.

A thrown pot can be burnished on the wheel using a metal kidney. This works best if the wheel is reversed so that the clay particles are compacted in the opposite direction.

This sequence shows the burnishing of a coil-built figure made of red clay, which is finished by smoking (*page 118*) and waxing. Luster stamping (*page 144*) is another interesting way of finishing, and incising (*page 30*) through the burnish makes a good contrast. There is no point in applying a glaze to burnished ware, since it will cover up all your hard work!

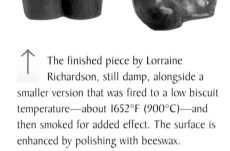

1 When leatherhard, the surface is burnished by compacting the clay particles in a polishing motion. The back of a spoon is a classic burnishing tool, and a smooth stone, a bone, or wooden modeling tool can be used. Smaller tools are needed to get into crevices and tight curves.

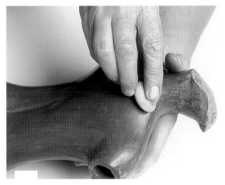

2 The clay should be on the dry side of leatherhard: too soft, and the tool just digs in and makes more marks; too dry, and it is difficult to change the clay surface. Take care not to crack the work, which becomes increasingly brittle at this stage. A little vegetable oil can combat dryness and help the tool to glide more easily across the surface.

↑ The finished piece by Lorraine Richardson, still damp, alongside a smaller version that was fired to a low biscuit temperature—about 1652°F (900°C)—and then smoked for added effect. The surface is enhanced by polishing with beeswax.

VARIATIONS

Left: *Burnished and smoke-fired vessel. The strength and purity of the form is enhanced by the subtle finish.*
ANTONIA SALMON

Center: *Pit-fired bottle made from porcelain and stoneware clay mixed with grog. Burnished and biscuit fired to 1922°F (1050°C) before pit firing.* ARDINE SPITTERS

Right: *Coil-built figure burnished and smoked before being wax polished; 24 in (70cm) high.*
LORRAINE RICHARDSON

MOLDS

MOLDS OFFER ENORMOUS POTENTIAL for decoration. They are widely used in the making process as a means of forming clay, but they can also be used to create an interesting surface. A relief image on a mold can be transferred to the surface of the clay, where it will appear in reverse. In this way, the mold becomes a printing block, and the clay receives the print.

Biscuit-fired clay and plaster are the two most frequently used materials. They are especially suitable because they are porous and absorb some moisture, enabling the clay to release easily from the mold as it dries. But many other materials provide good surfaces for carving; wood and linoleum, for example, are often used to print onto clay.

A mold can be time-consuming to produce, depending on its complexity, but once made it can be used many times over, allowing repeat patterning. Variations are possible also. By working into a basic cast, each print can be different from the next.

Molds are hugely versatile, as the following pages show, and they can be made from a multitude of materials such as clay, linoleum, plastic, wax, wood, plant parts, and other natural objects, even plaster itself (which must first be sealed with moldmakers' size).

USING PLASTER

Potters are often wary of using plaster, precisely because it does not mix well with clay. If even a small piece of plaster becomes embedded in the clay, it can cause "exploding" in the kiln. In fact, the problem is usually limited to a flake of clay popping off the surface of work during firing, but that, of course, is enough to spoil the piece. The use of plaster is always best confined to a designated area, but if that is not possible, meticulous cleaning up is essential to avoid contamination of the clay.

Having recognized these problems, it must be said that plaster is an amazingly useful material. It is inexpensive, can be poured over models of

BASIC TOOLBOX

Potters' plaster

Bucket and scales to weigh plaster 2.2 lb (1kg)

Casting boards

Suitable clay

Rolling pin

Craft knives

Modeling tools

Kidney palette

Sponges

Top: *Detail of mixed media panel using porcelain and glass. This piece was relief printed from plaster and colorwashed with iron oxide to accentuate the detail.* LES RUCINSKI

Center: *Bas-relief plaque colored with oxides. Fired to 1832°F (1000°C).* EDWARD POOLEY

Bottom: *Hand-thrown earthenware teapot with bee sprigs added, and slab-built stand with fruit sprigs.* SARAH MONK

AWKWARD OBJECT

If you cannot pour plaster over your chosen object to make a mold, try an interim process, using mold-making compounds such as silicone rubber or vinyl. A specialist sculptors' supplier will advise on appropriate materials and techniques for more complex objects.

almost any shape, and will take up incredibly fine detail. It can also be carved or incised more accurately than clay, and its shrinkage is minimal. Before mixing plaster for a mold, make a frame around the piece that is to form the mold. The plaster will be poured into the frame, so it must be carefully secured and thoroughly sealed.

A plaster mold should be dried thoroughly before use or it will be easily damaged. A drying cupboard can speed this up, but plaster will crack if it gets too hot.

Above: A lion's head mold made in the bas-relief technique from an original architectural detail. It is hollow behind and has a depth of about four inches (7.5cm). (See also page 39.)

MIXING PLASTER

TYPES OF PLASTER

Three kinds of plaster are commonly used for molds:

- Potters' plaster: the most universal and inexpensive.
- Dental plaster: a finer grade, suitable for more detailed work.
- High-density plasters: used widely in industry, these set very hard. They are the most durable, but less absorbent.

NB Builders' plaster is not suitable.

1 There is a ratio of plaster to water that works well, and the best way of achieving consistent results is to measure both every time. For potters' plaster, a mixture of 2.75 lb (1.25kg) of plaster to 1 quart (1 liter) of water is a good rule of thumb. The mixture can be strengthened by increasing the plaster, or softened by decreasing it. Follow the manufacturer's advice.

2 Begin with the water in a bucket, and gradually sprinkle the plaster into it, allowing it to soak for a minute or two until no dry patches are visible.

37

Below: Oxides and stoneware glazes are used to highlight the relief surface of this tile, which was made by rolling clay onto a textured, biscuit-fired surface. This is an example of the use of clay rather than plaster for moldmaking. RUTH BARKER

3 Now mix by hand without agitating too vigorously, which would introduce air. When the plaster is dispersed, the mixture becomes creamy and smooth.

4 Within about 5 minutes of stirring it begins to thicken and is then ready to pour. It is important to catch it at the right moment. Too early, and it can settle out, making the mix uneven, and liable to leak from any gaps. Too late, and it may not flow into crevices. As it sets, a chemical reaction occurs, giving off heat. It is said to have "cured" when it cools again.

Bas-relief

RELIEF MODELING IS ACHIEVED by building up with clay and perhaps also carving into the surface. Bas-relief is a shallow relief modeling technique, which is generally used for flat tile panels but can also be applied to curved surfaces. The technique demonstrated here involves three stages: modeling in bas-relief, making a mold from the model, and finally using the mold to produce a cast. The mold means that the plaque or image may be reproduced many times over.

YOU WILL NEED

Plaster

Wooden casting box

Soft clay

Modeling tools

1 A life drawing of a calf was the starting point for a panel in classical style. The piece begins with drawing on clay and is gradually built up until the modeler is satisfied with the final piece.

2 At this point it could be finished, hollowed a little from the back if too thick, dried, and fired. Here, though, a mold of the piece is made, so that more versions can be reproduced. For the purposes of mold making, the original piece is known as the "model."

3 Place a wooden casting box around the model and pour in the plaster. After 10–15 minutes, remove the casting box and turn the mold over. Remove the original clay model, which may be destroyed in the process. Allow the mold to dry completely before use.

4 Press soft clay into the mold. The way this is done can affect the finished surface. If a slab of clay is rolled out first and then pressed in, the surface will be smooth. Clay pressed in in pieces will leave tiny crease lines on the front of the cast, which can enhance the surface.

VARIATIONS

Left and center: *Terra cotta plaques, on the left, untreated, on the right, waxed.* EDWARD POOLEY

Right: *Modeling is a traditional method of applying decoration to a finished pot at the leatherhard stage. Modeling can be directly applied, can be built into the mold itself, or can be applied as a sprig (see page 40). Figurative modeling, as seen here on this very large plant pot, is classical in style and often reminiscent of architectural features and details such as stone carving.* WHICHFORD POTTERY

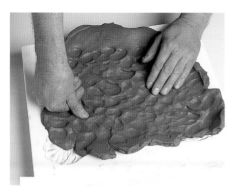

5 Push the clay very firmly into the mold so that it fills the crevices and takes up all the detail, exluding all air. Relatively soft clay will be easier to use for this process, known as press-molding.

6 Carefully scrape back the clay to the same level as the plaster mold. Do not dig into the clay, but the center can be slightly hollowed to ensure that the edges sit flat.

7 Within an hour or so, the clay will shrink and the cast should drop out easily. Place it on a flat surface and dry it slowly to avoid warping.

↑ This terra cotta plaque by Edward Pooley was fired to 2102°F (1150°C) and was finished with wax polish.

TIPS

- When making a mold, it is important that the model and the clay are able to part easily, so undercuts must be avoided and angles must be carefully checked to allow the model to free itself from the mold without tearing.

- Modeling is a technique requiring practice and is aided by drawing and observation from life.

- When adding pieces of clay to the surface be sure not to trap air pockets underneath as these will cause problems if the piece is to be fired.

- If the piece you make is too thick, hollow some clay out from the back to allow it to dry and fire more evenly.

- Try investigating surface finishes other than glaze, such as washes of oxide, which will not cover fine detail.

39

← The lion depicted here dates from the early 20th century. It was made by Stanley Bros. Brick Works in Nuneaton, England, and used as part of a decorative façade on buildings. A vinyl mold was taken from the original, and a plaster model was made from it. Then a plaster mold was made, pictured above left. The mold has been used to press clay into, and the resulting clay lion was attached to a circular plaque and fired to 2012°F (1100°C) without glaze.

Sprigging

SPRIGGING MAKES USE OF shallow molds into which clay is pressed. These can be biscuit-fired clay or plaster. A classic example of sprigging is the blue-and-white Jasperware made by Wedgwood: the white raised patterns applied to the blue body are sprigs.

The method for making sprigs is the same as for bas relief (*page 38*) but usually on a much smaller scale. A model is made—preferably on a nonporous background, such as a glazed tile or acrylic sheet—and plaster is poured over. When the mold is dry, soft clay can be pushed in. Instead of waiting until the clay shrinks and drops out, however, it is advisable to give it a little help. Pushing a piece of clay onto the back of the sprig until it sticks, and tugging gently, helps to free the cast from the mold. Eased out of the mold early, the sprig will still be damp enough to stick to the clay background. Score and slip both of the surfaces that are to be joined, in order to form a good bond, and be sure to exclude all possibility of air pockets. More delicate sprigs need careful handling, and only a light application of slip or water to make them adhere.

YOU WILL NEED

Object from which to make a sprig, a found object or something similar modeled from clay

Plaster or clay

Wet or leatherhard piece on which to apply sprigs

Slip for joining

USING A SHELL SPRIG

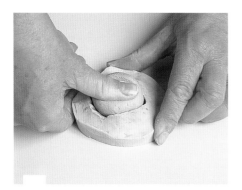

1 Clay is pushed into the mold. This mold was made from clay, just by pushing a shell into the clay and easing it out again. The mold was then biscuit fired.

2 A clay pad is attached, and the cast eased out, being careful not to damage or distort it. Sprigs should be attached while still quite soft. Being small they dry quickly, so this means working quite swiftly.

3 Casts of the shell with the mold. If several sprigs are made at a time, they should be kept damp in polythene, or covered with a damp cloth, until you are ready to use them.

4 Sprigs attached to the edges of a slab that will be used for a birdbath (see the finished piece, right). The piece was dried slowly to avoid distortion or warping.

← Birdbath, by Jo Connell: a thrown stem and press-molded dish with shell sprigs around the edge. Finished with a dry stoneware glaze.

WHEN A STAMP BECOMES A SPRIG

This sequence shows a blend of stamping (*see page 32*) and sprigging. A stamp is pushed into a pre-formed pad of clay and used to form leaves on a candlestick. Pressed out of the "mold," this motif becomes a sprig.

3 Slip is used to attach the wings to the bird and the leaves to the stem. These are modeled onto a candlestick, the main body of which was thrown on the wheel while coils formed the curvaceous stems. The modeled birds were then added to the stems.

1 The stamp is used to create leaves and wings from small pads of clay that have been rolled in the hand.

2 Two sprigs form the wings that appear on the final piece. They are joined together with a small amount of slip.

DELICATE SPRIGS

The finished candlestick, by Paul Young, in earthenware with colored glazes. Fired to 2048°F (1120°C).

This delicate sprig mold was made from plaster. The model was made from clay, in bas relief, and plaster was poured over to make the mold.

41

VARIATIONS

Left: Lidded storage jar with sheaves of corn sprigs. Biscuit fired, glazed with an opaque tin glaze, and fired again to 2048°F (1120°C).
STEVE MATTISON

Center and right: Platter with bee sprigging and stamped decoration. The bee antennae were made by extruding china clay from a cake piping bag. The bug eggcup holder has a variety of sprigging including bugs, berries, and leaves.
SARAH MONK

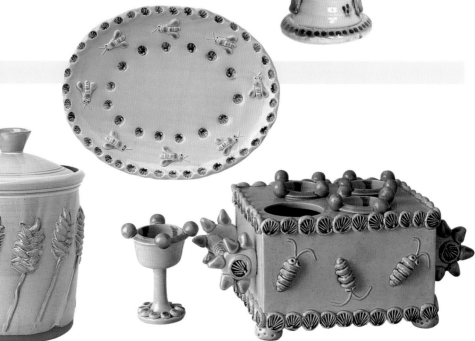

Molds for Relief Printing

THE BAS-RELIEF TECHNIQUE (*see page 38*) showed how clay can be pressed into a mold to take impressions from plaster. In this sequence, clay is pressed onto a plaster surface that was carved instead of moldmade. The imagery here is much finer and makes use of the precision and delicacy possible with incisions into plaster. Such an effect would be difficult to achieve by modeling. When using molds in this way it is essential to remember that a mirror image will result—so any lettering on the slab (which will become the "mold") must be done in reverse.

YOU WILL NEED

Plaster slab

Sharp tools for carving

Cloth

Soft clay

IMAGES ON PLASTER

1 Drawing images onto plaster gives accurate and delicate effects. Try using a metal sgraffito tool on a smooth plaster surface.

2 Roll out a thin slab of clay on a cloth and trim it to size—the clay will adhere to the cloth so can be easily handled without stretching it out of shape. Press it down onto the plaster firmly but with care—the cloth will prevent fingermarks on the clay.

3 Carefully peel the clay back off the plaster block to reveal the raised print. This method combines the concepts of moldmaking and printing.

VARIATIONS

Left: Press-molded vessel. Two halves made from a carved mold, painted with colored slips. Both color and texture are transferred to the clay surface. HEATHER MORRIS

Center left: Porcelain plaque created by the technique above, this shows the effectiveness of unglazed, uncolored porcelain. LAURA VICKERS

Center and center right: Two tiles. A design was drawn into the plaster and the clay pressed down on it to form a reverse (raised) print, which has been enhanced with underglaze color. CHRISTINE GEDDES

Right top: A small panel of bas-relief is inset into a frame of printed clay and is attached carefully with slip. Colored with iron oxide and fired to 2102°F (1150°C). LES RUCINSKI

Far right: Lino-printed jug. The artist was trained as a printmaker and transfers print techniques to clay surfaces. Colors are first built up using thin layers of slip, on a clay slab, then a roller is used to roll ink onto a lino cut. The lino is registered with the colored slip and pressure applied. The slabs are then used to build a three-dimensional form. JULIETTE GODDARD

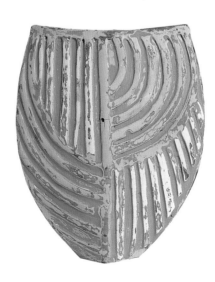

INTAGLIO: RELIEF PRINTING FROM PLASTER

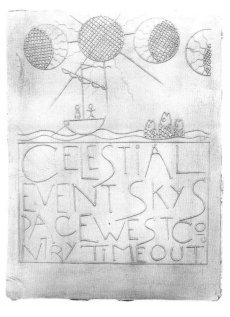

1 As before, a cloth is used as a backing for a thin slab of clay as it is pressed down onto a carved plaster block. Smooth firmly, being careful not to blur the print. Here we use porcelain, a smooth, white clay that is ideal for delicate images printed in this way.

2 The thin slab can be formed into a three-dimensional piece or remain flat. It can be colored in different ways but here a light wash of underglaze color was applied.

↑ The finished piece by Les Rucinski, lightly sponged with underglaze color.

← This plaster mold was taken from a large leaf and shows the degree of detail that can be achieved using this method.

43

DRAWING, PAINTING, AND PRINTING

THE RANGE OF MARKS MADE by drawing, painting, and printing is vast, and specific techniques are demonstrated in other sections of the book (sgraffito, incising, brushwork with slip, etc). Clay can, of course, be drawn, painted, or printed on at different stages of the making process. Here we look at raw, unfired clay. Having examined some ways of altering the surface of clay, we begin to introduce more color, and to look more closely at the possibilities offered by printing.

An almost endless variety of marks is possible at the clay stage, and there are diverse techniques for making them, as this section illustrates. There are, however, a few general guidelines. Working on a flat surface is much easier than working in three dimensions, especially when printing. The surface of your "canvas" needs to be receptive. It will be difficult to paint or print onto a textured surface or one that is ridged with throwing rings, for example. A printed surface is extremely fragile and prone to marking or smudging, especially when freshly done. But printing at the clay stage gives the advantage of flexibility—the clay is still pliable enough to be formed into a three-dimensional object.

CHOOSING A SUITABLE CLAY

Your choice of clay will depend on several factors—the kind of marks to be made, the brightness of color required, the size of the piece and the making method used, and the temperature to which it will be fired. Your ceramics supplier's catalogue will list a variety of clays with their firing temperatures and working properties and sample bags may even be available. With experience you will find a clay to suit your particular needs.

If delicate or accurate marks are required, a smooth clay will give the finest surface on which to paint or incise, and for printing it will provide a better contact than textured clay. Porcelain is an obvious choice, but fine white earthenware clays are available that will not demand so high a temperature and therefore offer a brighter color palette.

For slab building, a relatively well grogged clay will be easier to handle and more resilient to warping and splitting at the joins. For wall panels and tiles, a grogged clay will be more likely to remain flat during drying and firing. Paper clay is worth considering here too, as it is easy to handle and can be used thinly.

Strongly stained clay such as terra cotta can provide a warm-colored base (see its effective use on page 46) but will obviously have an influence on the slips and stains applied over it, unless these are very strong or opaque. Buff clay will similarly have a muting effect on the fired color.

BASIC TOOLBOX

Sgraffito tools

Colored slips

For monoprint: sheet of glass or acrylic, water-based medium, and print roller

For screen print: silk screen and squeegee, newspaper, and slips

Suitable clay

Optional: casting slip for painting into molds

Top: *Slabs of white stoneware clay are screen printed with underglaze colors and then assembled. They are biscuit fired to 2120°F (1160°C) and clear glazed.* FLEUR HARVEY

Center: *Porcelain vases, slab built and inlaid with slip. Glazed inside and fired to 2372°F (1300°C) in a gas kiln.* JUDE JELFS

Bottom: *Press-molded piece, clay added to the basic form and built up. Decorated with oxides, color stains, and velvet underglaze.* CHRISTY KEENEY

STONEWARE GLAZES
2282°F (1250°C)

Clear Gloss

Potash Feldspar	30
Flint	28
Whiting	15
Barium Carbonate	10
China Clay	10
Zinc Oxide	4
Talc	3

Matte Transparent

Cornish Stone	60
Dolomite	20
China Clay	20

Matte White

Nepheline Syenite	34
China Clay	20
Flint	18
Dolomite	14
Whiting	8
Zinc Oxide	6

EARTHENWARE GLAZES
(see note on metal release on page 87)

Satin Matte *2102°F (1150°C)*

Lead Bisilicate	40
Feldspar	25
China Clay	18
Whiting	12
Flint	5

(increase China Clay to make a more matte finish)

Clear Gloss
Approx 1940–2012°F (1060–1100°C)

Lead Bisilicate	72
Ball Clay	15
Flint	9
Whiting	4

Cream Clear Gloss*
Approx 1976–2048°F (1080–1120°C)

Lead Bisilicate	80
Potash Feldspar	10
Red Clay	10

The addition of 2% Bentonite makes this suitable for glazing leatherhard clay and omitting the biscuit firing.

*(*after Paul Young)*

COLOR

Colored slips are discussed on page 54 and the basic recipes given there can be adapted by experiment to give a wide range of hues. Oxides and underglaze colors can be applied neat to a raw clay surface, but when dry they are fragile and can be rubbed off when handled. To prevent this, a little white clay can be added to the neat color to make a concentrated slip, which will adhere more readily as the pot dries.

Various colored pigments or *engobes* (*see* Unglazed Pigments, *page 96*, for recipes) can be painted directly onto unfired clay and fired with or without a glaze.

GLAZES

In the box, left, are recipes for clear and matte glazes at both earthenware and stoneware temperatures. If applied relatively thinly these can form unobtrusive glaze coverings over a previously colored (painted or printed) surface. Good, reliable, clear glazes are also easily obtainable ready mixed from your supplier.

It is worth remembering that the color beneath a glaze is affected by the composition of the glaze itself, and some glazes give a better color response than others.

Above: Slip-cast porcelain vase decorated with slip painted into the mold itself, a form of monoprinting. Fired to 2282°F (1250°C) without glaze. SUE DYER

Below: *Porcelain vessel with monoprinted slips. Slip is brushed onto newspaper, dried, and images scratched through. The print is transferred to the leatherhard pot, which is then biscuit fired. Matte glazes are brushed on and the piece fired again to 2102°F (1150°C).* FIONA THOMPSON

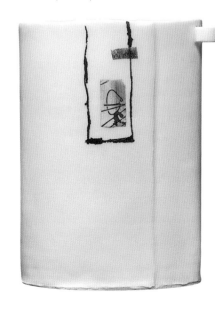

DRAWING, PAINTING, AND PRINTING

CHAPTER 1

Drawing and Painting on Clay

MANY TECHNIQUES IN THIS BOOK involve drawing and painting on clay. Ceramics is an extremely versatile and expressive medium and gives great scope for developing a personal style, as the examples show.

This coil-built piece, made from terra cotta clay, is decorated in free and graphic style at the leatherhard stage. A combination of colored slips, brushstrokes, and sgraffito methods (*see page 68*) are effectively combined on a three-dimensional surface.

YOU WILL NEED

A selection of tools for incising and sgraffito

Brushes, various

Colored slips

1 A thin coating of colored slips is applied with a broad, soft brush.

2 Layers of color are built up. The colors vary at this stage, but after firing they will look similar and will give a shaded effect.

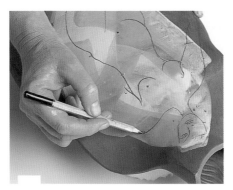

3 A pencil is used to sgraffito a line drawing through the slips.

A completed piece by Lorraine Richardson, showing the subtlety of color. Here the background slip was scraped away to emphasize the outline of the figure. It was fired to 2012°F (1100°C) and polished with beeswax.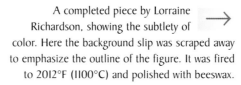

VARIATIONS

Left: *Bowl full of color and movement decorated with slip resist and sgraffito.* JEAN PAUL LANDREAU

Center: *Earthenware bowl with colored slips and sgraffito.* VIVIENNE ROSS

Right: *Entitled "Eve in Yellow Trousers," this jug is slab-built earthenware decorated with vitreous slips and glazed inside.* JUDE JELFS

SLIP-DECORATED BOWL

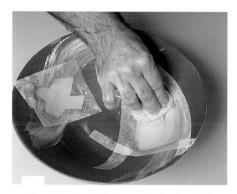

1 Apply a dark slip to the leatherhard clay and allow to become touch dry. Now, apply paper strips and hold them there by dampening them lightly. Wipe away the dark slip outside the paper strips leaving a light background on which to paint.

2 Using a soft oriental brush, paint yellow slip in the space defined by the paper stencil. Drying can be speeded up by using a hair dryer. The slip resist method is seen in more detail on page 76.

3 Splatter red slip onto parts of the surface using a toothbrush, to add to the richness and depth of the design.

4 Remove stencils when touch dry. Incise lines through the slip in sgraffito style (*see page 68*), just deeply enough to reveal the white clay beneath. These white lines show up in sharp contrast after firing.

The finished piece, by Jean Paul Landreau. It was biscuit fired then covered in a transparent earthenware glaze and fired again to 2048°F (1120°C).

CALLIGRAPHY

Drawing into clay is an excellent way of making a written statement, and presentation plates can make lovely gifts for posterity. Examples can be found throughout history, from narrative scenes on Ancient Greek vases depicting myths and legends, to portraits of monarchy on early delftware and slipware. Lettering is a natural extension of the graphic use of tools and brushes to enhance a ceramic surface.

Cut the tip of a paintbrush to a chisel point to create calligraphic writing. Draw the letters through the slip, using the sgraffito technique.

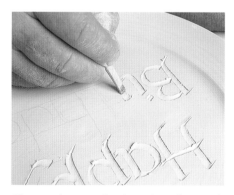

Writing around the rim of a plate or dish has often been used for commemorative purposes. The contrasting color enhances the design.

Alternatively, incise the clay without the use of color. A translucent colored glaze would complete this porcelain plate.

47

Monoprinting

A MONOPRINT OWES ITS NAME to its uniqueness. Color is transferred from one surface to another, so the print can only be made once. Subsequent pressings may produce a similar though fainter print, but it will not be the same as the first. Monoprinting offers plenty of scope for relatively quick and easy experimentation. Here are three methods of monoprinting on soft clay.

YOU WILL NEED

Sheet of glass or acrylic

Water-based screen print medium

Print roller

Stiff paintbrush

Wooden modeling tool

Rolling pin

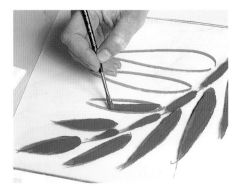

1 Make a simple drawing on paper and place it under glass. This acts as a guide for freehand painting on the glass. Here, red iron oxide is used with a water-based medium to give a sticky consistency. The paint does not "flow" easily but stays where it is put. Such sticky paint does not allow for detailed brushwork, but try experimenting with various mixtures.

METHOD I • FREEHAND PAINTING

This method makes use of a simple painting technique onto a shiny, non-absorbent surface. This is transferred to clay before it is dry, so you will need to work with reasonable speed. Here, only one color is used, but with care a multicolored design could be achieved. Fortunately, mistakes can easily be wiped off the glass.

2 Make some sgraffito lines through the painting, but do not allow the oxide mixture to dry.

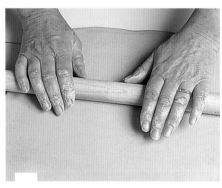

3 When the design is finished, lower a slab of clay carefully onto the surface and press it down. Apply a rolling pin very gently on the back of the clay, so as not to smudge the image.

4 Carefully peel the clay back without letting your fingers touch the printed area. The image is transferred in a kind of blotting process. The surface is fragile, but it could be carefully formed using a mold, or gently manipulated in the same way as the slab-built musical wave on page 53.

↑ The finished tile, glazed with a matte white stoneware and fired to 2282°F (1250°C).

VARIATIONS

Left: *Monoprinted slab. Layers of monoprint, stencil, and linoprint were built up and when dry enough a sheet of newspaper was placed on a slab and a drawing made on the back creating the pink lines. Fired to 2300°F (1260°C).*
CAROL WHEELER

Center left: *Colander image, printed off newspaper on which layers of slips have been painted, allowing each layer to dry before building up the next.*
JO CONNELL

Center right: *Layers of slips were built up on newspaper, starting with the dark fish outline and ending with the* blue/gray background. When the print is transferred to clay, the image is reversed so that the fish appears on top of the background.
JO CONNELL

Right: *Porcelain vessel using monoprinted slips and pigments.*
FIONA THOMPSON

METHOD 2 • SINGLE COLOR

This method is very similar to the last, but here a design is drawn into a solid background, removing color instead of applying it to the glass plate.

1 Begin with a shiny surface, such as acrylic or glass—known as the "plate." Disperse color on the plate with a print roller. The color here is underglaze mixed with a water-friendly medium to the consistency of syrup.

2 Draw a design into the sticky surface by removing the color with a broad-tipped tool, palette knife, or cotton bud.

3 Press a clay slab gently onto the plate, taking care not to smudge the impression by any sideways movement.

4 When the slab is peeled off we can see that some of the color is transferred. A second print would be possible but would not be as strong. Trim, form, and dry the delicate surface without touching the print.

The slab is biscuit fired and then glazed with transparent earthenware glaze.

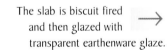

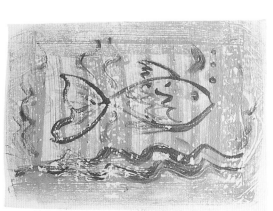

METHOD 3 • USING SLIPS

In this method, slips are painted onto paper and printed onto clay. Alternatively, clay can be applied to layers of slip built up on a sheet of paper. Prints can also be taken from slips painted on plaster. The slip in this example is made from 50:50 china clay and ball clay, and stained with underglaze colors or body stains.

1 Build up a design, using intensely colored slips. Paint each color onto a strip of newspaper and allow it to dry slightly until the sheen goes. Then apply it face down onto a clay slab and rub the back lightly with your fingers.

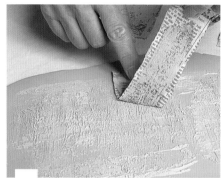

2 Peel the newspaper back, discard it, and apply the next layer. Gradually build up the individual prints in as many layers and directions as you need.

↑ The final piece was fired to 2300°F (1260°C) in an electric kiln without a glaze. The method could be used to construct curved or three-dimensional forms, provided care is taken not to smudge the printed surface.

3 The textured surface is reminiscent of peeling paintwork, and conveys an "aged" effect. Trim the slab, tear the edges, and drape the clay into a press-mold to dry.

50

VARIATIONS

Right: Hollow vessel made from slabs of terra cotta clay printed from relief plaster molds coated with slips. Color and texture are transferred to the surface (detail of similar piece, below). HEATHER MORRIS

Far right: This paper-clay plaque is printed with slips off textured plaster surface, employing the technique of relief printing from plaster as well as monoprinting. HEATHER MORRIS

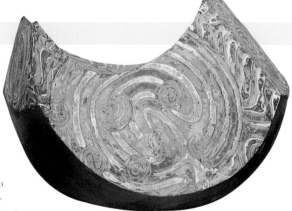

Monoprinting From Plaster

THIS METHOD USES MOLDS to transfer color from a plaster surface to a clay surface—a form of monoprinting (*see page 48*). Only one print at a time can be made by this technique. It produces an interesting layered effect and beautiful depth of color where the pattern is applied.

The process demonstrated here uses slip casting, but the technique can be adapted to press-molding from two- and three-dimensional plaster molds. The artist uses porcelain because it is particularly well suited to incising, giving clean, sharp lines and a bright color response.

YOU WILL NEED

Colored slips
Molds (see page 36)
Porcelain casting slip
Brushes
Craft knife

1 Paint the colored slips into the mold itself. They will dry quickly but must not be allowed to flake off the surface. Build up several layers. Remember that the first color applied will appear on the surface of the design when it transfers to the clay.

2 Strap the two halves of the mold together using strong, wide rubber bands, and pour in porcelain casting slip.

3 Allow the slip to cast for the appropriate time, drain it, and leave it to dry for an hour or two. Take the mold apart to reveal the colored slip design.

4 Scrape back to neaten the surface, then incise a few lines with a craft knife or excise knife to sharpen the design.

5 Fill the incised lines with contrasting colored slips, making sure the grooves are full, then scraping back once the slip has stiffened (*see* Inlaying Slips, *page 74*).

The finished piece: Iris vase, by Sue Dyer, fired to 2264°F (1240°C). →

VARIATIONS

Below:*White porcelain vase with painted inlaid slips.* SUE DYER

Screen Printing

SCREEN PRINTING IS BEST KNOWN for its use on paper, but it is also a wonderful way to apply designs to a clay surface. Although associated with industrially produced ceramics, it can be equally successful in the studio. Like most print methods it can be used at different stages of making. Here we apply a screen print to a wet clay slab.

YOU WILL NEED

Silk screen

Squeegee

Newspaper

Slips

Clay slabs

PRINTING WITH SLIPS

Buy a screen from a specialist supplier, or make your own from polyester mesh tightly stretched and stapled over a strong wooden frame. A tool such as a canvas stretcher is useful for this—or an extra pair of hands! Screens were traditionally made of silk, but nowadays a tough monofilament polyester is preferred. You can obtain this from a screen print supplier. Meshes vary, and slips call for a fairly coarse grade: about 40T (threads per inch).

Screen printing is essentially a resist technique (*see page 76*). This demonstration uses the stencil method. It allows considerable control, although it is less accurate than the photo silk screen approach (*see page 138*), and the stencil itself has a limited life—here, it is used only once.

↑ Colors are not what they seem! The buff clay fires white, the pinkish slip fires blue. Finished bowl by Carol Wheeler in stoneware with a matte white glaze.

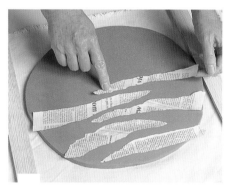

1 Prepare a slab of clay. It must be absolutely flat, and not too wet. Arrange strips of torn newspaper on the clay. They will resist the slip, and must extend beyond the edges of the planned design. Wooden slats raise the screen slightly above the clay to prevent the two from actually touching. The screen will stretch to allow sufficient contact.

2 The slip used here is thick and was well sieved. You need enough color at the top edge of the screen to carry across the entire design. Pull the slip toward you slowly with the squeegee, using even pressure. Hold the squeegee at 45°, so that the sharper edge of the rubber blade forces the slip through the mesh. Squeegee once, but if this seems insufficient, make a second pull in the same direction. (Reversing the pull can move the screen slightly and blur the print.) An extra pair of hands can be useful to hold the screen firm.

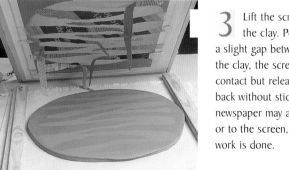

3 Lift the screen carefully off the clay. Positioned to leave a slight gap between the mesh and the clay, the screen stretches into contact but releases and snaps back without sticking. The newspaper may adhere to the clay or to the screen, but by then its work is done.

Screen Printing With Pigments

SCREEN PRINTING CAN BE DONE with pigments other than slip at the wet clay stage. In this example, a black underglaze color, mixed with a water-based screen-printing medium, is used to print directly onto an even slab of wet or leatherhard clay. The color is first blended to a smooth and sticky paste with a palette knife. Experience will dictate how thick to make the color—not too runny, but still thin enough to be forced through the screen.

The musical image was made by the photo silk screen process (*see page 138*).

YOU WILL NEED

Silk screen

Squeegee

Photo silk screen facilities (see page 138)

Underglaze color, water-based medium

Palette knife

Soft slabs of a suitable clay

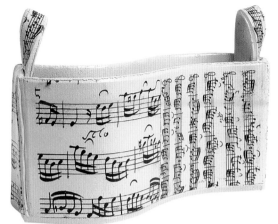

"Musical wave," by Jo Connell. Fired to 2102°F (1150°C) with a satin matte transparent glaze, allowing the print to show through.

1 Prepare a slab of clay and place it carefully for screen printing, with the wooden slats positioned, as before, to raise the screen slightly above the clay.

2 The squeegee must fit the image—that is, it must be very slightly wider than the image, but not so wide that it catches on the edges of the screen.

3 Lift the screen with care. The printed slab of clay is highly susceptible to damage at this stage.

VARIATIONS

Left: *Photo-screen printed tile, using gray slip onto white clay and coated with clear glaze after biscuit firing.*
JO CONNELL

Right: *Vase screen printed with pigments.*
FLEUR HARVEY

4 The advantage of printing onto wet clay is evident here—it is still flexible enough to be shaped, though the printed surface must not be touched.

53

DRAWING, PAINTING, AND PRINTING

CHAPTER

SLIPS

SLIP HAS BEEN USED as a means of coloring and decorating ceramics for centuries. As soon as potters discovered clays of different colors, it was found that clay mixed with water made a useful coating for the surface of a pot. Slip is simply a mixture of clay, water, and sometimes a pigment—such as an oxide or stain—though other materials are occasionally added to help it fit the clay body to which it is applied. The mixture should be well stirred and sieved before use.

When slip is mixed to a thick consistency it is possible to change the surface color of a pot with one application. In this way, it provides a solid colored background for paint or glaze, and is an inexpensive way of making a common dark clay appear white. When slip is thinner, it gives interesting effects, allowing the base clay to show through, and different layers of color and texture can be built up. Possibilities for decoration at this early stage are enormously varied.

When first applied and still wet, a coating of slip can be marbled with other colors, combed through with tools or fingers, brushed to create a textured surface, and so on. This allows a spontaneous approach to decoration, which can be applied directly and fluently. As slip dries, it lends itself to more controlled methods of drawing, painting, and incising, and fine detail is achievable.

BASIC TOOLBOX

Clay for making slips (see recipes)

Oxides and stains

Brushes, slip trailer, sgraffito and combing tools

Wax: hot wax or water-based type

Sieve (80s mesh or thereabouts)

See individual techniques for materials and small tools (e.g. tobacco juice, sponges, newsprint)

Above: *A wide variety of tools are used for applying slip, including sponges, slip trailers, and brushes.*

Top: *The left-hand form was carved and inlaid with textured slip, then painted with gold luster and fired again. The right-hand form was inlaid with two slips, blue and textured black.* CAROLINE WHYMAN
Center: *Earthenware pasta bowl, white clay, decorated with a single bold brushstroke of dark slip, and clear glazed.* JONNA BEHRENS
Below: *Slab-built vase in earthenware, with slip-trailed and paper-stencil decoration.* MARK DALLY

Left: *Limoges porcelain, thrown and turned on the wheel and decorated with brushed and trailed colored slips.* KOCHEVET BEN-DAVID

Above: Slip-decorated plate with cut rim decorated with two layers of glaze; a copper semi-matte, and a cobalt semi-matte. JOHN CALVER

Left: Sieving ensures that the slip is of even consistency and helps to disperse any color that has been added. An 80s mesh should be fine enough for most slips. Higher numbers denote a finer mesh.

The use of resists (*see page 76*) with slip is another way of creating areas of contrasting color.

Many potters choose to decorate exclusively with slip. Some use a limited palette associated with traditional country pottery: white, cream, brown, black, and occasionally greens and blues—covered perhaps with a clear or honey-colored transparent glaze. Domestic ware of this kind has been widely used and loved over the centuries, and its warmth and familiarity have a particular appeal. Other potters may choose a more contemporary palette, making use of the range of vivid stains now available, or they may use subtle pastel colors to give ethereal effects. Slip colors are richer and brighter when coated with a clear glaze, but at higher temperatures slip can be left without glaze if a matte surface is preferred.

Vitreous slip is made from a clay that becomes glasslike at higher temperatures and forms a slight sheen on the pot. Some naturally occurring clays do this, but fluxes can be added to cause slips to vitrify—borax frit is often used for this. Vitreous slips and engobes are discussed further on page 96. "Slip glazes" are glazes with a high proportion of clay, so they can be applied at the green (unfired) stage and without the need of biscuit firing—these often lend themselves to sgraffito, combing, or wax-resist decoration.

55

BASIC RECIPES FOR COLORED SLIPS

As a white slip base, ball clay alone can be used. On some bodies, ball clay may peel or flake off due to its high shrinkage. In this case, try adding 20–50% china clay, or use your usual clay body itself as a base.

The colors listed will result when the slips are coated with a transparent glaze.

Suggested upper and lower limits of additions are indicated.

Add to the slip, by dry weight:	Amount:	Color:
Cobalt Oxide/Carbonate	0.5–2%	blue
Copper Oxide/Carbonate	1–5%	green (will be buff without a glaze)
Iron Oxide	3–12%	cream to dark brown
Manganese Dioxide	5–12%	browns
Nickel Oxide	2–5%	brown/gray

Combinations of the above can of course be mixed.

Red Iron Oxide	8%	
+Cobalt Oxide	8%	
+Manganese Dioxide	8%	black

Body stains in the ratio 5–15% give a wide range of colors. Red clay can be used alone or with the addition of up to 30% Red Iron Oxide to strengthen the color. It can also be used as a base for a darker blue, or for black. Home-dug clay is often a low-firing, iron-bearing clay that can be useful as a slip.

Above: Hand-thrown bowl decorated with an oak leaf design created using sponging, glazing, dipping, and detailed brushwork. RALPH JANDRELL

Pouring

POURING IS A SIMPLE and effective way of applying slip, which enhances the forms it coats.

The object is held firmly over a bucket while a pitcher of slip is poured over it. A natural "curtain" of slip results in a fluid curve caused by the pouring action that complements a rounded form.

When designing a form to be decorated in this way, remember that it must be held confidently in one hand for a few minutes while the other hand does the pouring and excess slip is allowed to drain off. It will be much easier if there is a substantial footring to hold at the base of the pot. Some forms, such as a round-based spherical bottle, would be impossible to grip but could be stood as slip is poured on.

YOU WILL NEED

Hot wax or water-based wax

Brush for wax

Jug or bowl and contrasting slips

Leatherhard pot to decorate

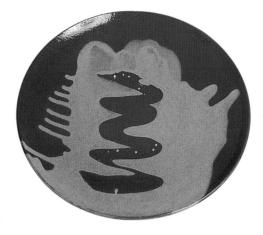

↑ A finished piece by John Commane. Bowl with earthenware honey glaze applied over white slip on red clay body.

1 Wax resist brushwork (*see page 64*), using hot wax, is applied to a bowl made of red clay.

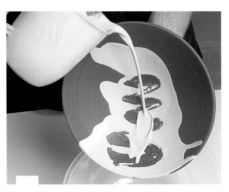

2 White slip is gently poured over the the bowl, which is held at an angle to prevent the slip pooling in the center.

3 The slip is shaken from side to side to encourage decorative runs. A bowl beneath catches the excess slip as it runs off.

VARIATIONS

Left: *Salt-glazed jar with poured slip and combed decoration.*
NICK SOMERVILLE
Right: *The plate was held vertically while colored slips were poured to decorative effect. Clear glaze was later applied. Earthenware, fired to 2102°F (1150°C).* JOHN COMMANE

Dipping

DIPPING, LIKE POURING, is a useful way of applying a dense and even coating of slip. The form must lend itself to easy handling. A thrown pot may be more easily held if it remains attached to a throwing bat and is wired off later. Always make sure that the bucket is wide enough and that there is sufficient depth of slip. The pot must not be allowed to touch the bottom or sides. Fingermarks are best rectified immediately while the slip is still fluid enough to heal over the marks.

In this example, dipping is used for decorative effect, and the dip lines follow the form of the piece.

YOU WILL NEED

Leatherhard pot to decorate
Bucket or bowl
Slip

↑ An alternative method of dipping is shown here where a cylinder that has been brushed with wax resist is dipped into slip (*see page 76*).

1 The vase is first dipped sideways to apply a "bib" of slip on the side. Lift the piece out carefully to avoid touching the sides of the bowl.

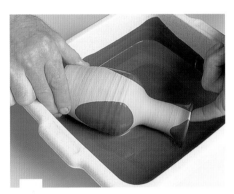

2 The vase is dipped again on the bib and then on the neck. Stand up carefully, avoiding fingermarks and not allowing runs to develop.

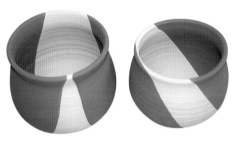

↑ Dipped pots, unfired. Dramatic effects can be achieved with this simple technique, but care and pouring practice are needed to get clean lines.

57

VARIATIONS

Left: *Tea bowl. Terra cotta clay dipped rim first into white slip and decorated with sgraffito and colored glazes.*
PAUL YOUNG

Center: *Mug with dipped rim. At the leatherhard stage the sgraffito design was drawn through the white slip, and after firing a honey glaze was applied over the decorated area.*
MOLLY ATTRILL

Right: *Reduction-fired stoneware jar with dipped slip beneath.*
DEREK EMMS

Slip Trailing

SLIP TRAILING IS USUALLY done with a rubber tool in the form of a bulb with a detachable nozzle, though many types of slip trailer exist. It is possible to improvise with plastic bottles and commercial packaging, but a customized tool can provide greater control.

YOU WILL NEED

Slip-trailer tool
Slip
Leatherhard item to decorate
Banding wheel

↑ Finished piece by Paul Young. After completing the slip trailing, the bowl was biscuit fired and some of the defined areas filled in with colored glazes, rather like tube lining, before being fired again to earthenware temperature, 2008°F (1100°C).

FLUENT LINES

Slip for trailing should be fairly thick in consistency and well sieved. For maximum fluency, practice first. This can be done on a sheet of plastic without wasting the slip. Load the trailer as fully as possible, shaking the slip down into the nozzle to avoid airlocks, which would spoil the flow of the lines. Squeeze evenly and steadily to produce a continuous flow of slip. After practice, your slip trailer will become as deft a drawing tool as a pencil or brush.

Trailing on a background of leatherhard clay or relatively dry slip results in raised lines. Other slips can be used later to fill the gaps, or after biscuit firing the areas between the lines can be filled with colored glazes. Trailing on a wet slip coating background will sink in more.

Tube lining is a process related to slip trailing, but is usually done on biscuit-fired ware with a special mixture more related to glaze than to slip. Colored glazes are then infilled between the raised lines, which can be darker or lighter than the trails of slip, and then re-fired. This technique was a popular method of decoration on Victorian tiles, and Moorcroft Pottery has made it a specialty.

↑ An example of Moorcroft pottery, showing their characteristic use of tube-lining decoration.

VARIATIONS

Near left: *Slip-trailed dish. Transparent cream earthenware glaze over brown background with white slip trailing.* PAUL YOUNG
Left top: *Detail showing white slip on red clay with clear glaze.*
Left bottom: *Limoges porcelain thrown and turned on the wheel, then decorated with brushed and trailed colored slips.* KOCHEVET BEN-DAVID
Center: *Slab-built earthenware envelope vase with slip-trailed decoration.* MARK DALLY
Right: *Slip-trailed pitcher with colored glazes.* NIEK HOOGLAND
Far right: *Pitcher with a clear ash glaze over white slip and dark slip trailed over.* WILLI SINGLETON

1 The leatherhard bowl is centered on a banding wheel, and lines of slip are trailed on while the wheel is moving.

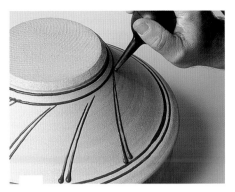

2 The bowl could be marked out lightly in pencil to give guidance, but here the slip trailing is done by eye—the result of a great deal of practice.

3 The pattern is built up using fluid lines and with a sure and steady hand. Here, only black slip is being used, though of course any color combination is possible.

4 The pattern is repeated on the inside. Plan the spacing before you start work so that the pattern is even all the way round.

5 Many potters feel that if their work is being handled, the inside and outside are of equal importance. Decorating all facets of the bowl, including the inside of the footring, makes it a truly three-dimensional piece and a pleasure to handle. It will even look good upside down on the draining board!

Feathering

This delicate effect is named for its feather-like pattern—and a feather can be used for dragging the slip.

A steady hand is needed for feathering, and fine control of the slip trailer, the tool that holds the slip. The technique can be used with slips of any color, but here we chose traditional black, with white lines and a honey glaze. Feathering is considerably more difficult to achieve on a three-dimensional piece, but it can be done. Many fine examples exist from the 18th century—notably some "owl" pitchers that have a fine surface pattern combed to simulate feathers.

YOU WILL NEED

Two colors of slip
Slip trailer
Jug for pouring
Feather or thin flexible stick or needle
Leatherhard bowl or slab for decorating

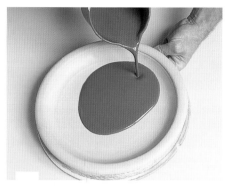

1 Pour a background of the black slip (it appears brown until fired) onto a leatherhard, flat-bottomed platter of white clay. Tip out the excess and clean the rim.

2 Trail parallel lines onto the background, using a white slip. Maintain an even pressure on the slip trailer, which should be kept full with the slip shaken down to the nozzle. A steady hand is needed here and mistakes are easily made—if this happens, try marbling to hide the problem!

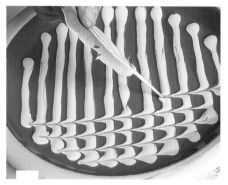

3 Use a feather to drag the slip in one direction, keeping the lines at equal distances apart. If mistakes are made the slip can be wiped off and you can begin again, but the pot will get softer and will be more liable to distort or collapse.

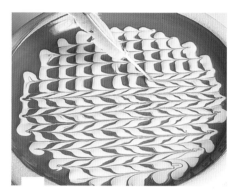

4 Now drag the slip in the other direction to create a feather-like effect—a technique similar to that used for frosting on cakes.

↑ Finished piece by Paul Young. The black and white slips are darkened and enriched by a traditional honey glaze of 3% red iron oxide in a clear earthenware glaze.

VARIATIONS

Below: *A detail of the effect of a honey glaze applied over black-and-white feathered marbling.*

Below right: *Plate, feathered in black and white with an earthenware honey glaze.* MOLLY ATTRILL

Marbling

VERY SIMILAR TO FEATHERING, marbling is another technique with its roots in traditional country pottery. Marbling begins by applying a coat of slip to a leatherhard pot—usually a dish or other simple form.

Throughout the decorating and drying process the plate remains on a wooden board. The heavy coating of slip necessary for this effect softens the clay dramatically, so it is liable to collapse unless it is supported. If the form is press-molded—a dish, for example—leave it in the mold throughout so that it will not distort, and remove it only when it has stiffened.

When dried again to a leatherhard state, the piece can be cleaned, and any smudges or drips of slip on the rim can be removed with a sponge or scraped away.

YOU WILL NEED
Two colors of slip
Slip trailer
Leatherhard bowl or slab

1 Begin with a background of liquid slip, in the same way as feathering. Then apply random dots of white slip.

2 Rock the plate to allow the slips to run together. The consistency of the slip is important and practice is needed to achieve the desired effect. Bold patterns will result at this early stage, becoming finer and more mingled with continued movement.

3 It is your decision when to stop! More movement will continue to blend the slip, and the lines will be less defined.

↑ Finished piece by Paul Young. Brown and white marbled slips with clear earthenware glaze.

61

VARIATIONS

Below: *Detail of blue and white marbled slips with a clear stoneware glaze.*
Center and right: *Two plates showing* *the fluid use of slips, trailed and marbled. Clear earthenware glaze over colored slips.* GABRIELLE RUCINSKI

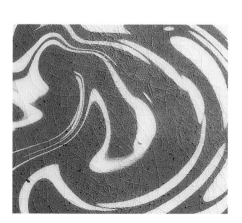

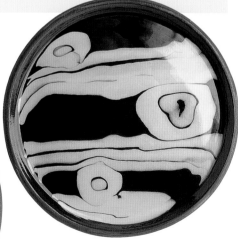

Spotting

SPOTTING IS A VERSATILE technique that can be achieved with a variety of tools, and functions well with other forms of decoration.

Spotting can be done with a finger, a slip trailer, or any tool that dispenses the right amount of slip and gives the desired kind of mark. The marks can be raised or they can be relatively level, depending upon the background to which they are applied. Like trailing, spotting gives interesting effects that can be used in conjunction with other decoration ideas. In this example, spotting methods are used to build up a pattern using colored slips on a white clay background.

YOU WILL NEED
Colored slips
Slip trailer
Leatherhard pot

↑ The finished jug, by Paul Young, with spotted slip decoration and stoneware glaze.

1 The slips need to be relatively thick in consistency to prevent them from running. Large spots of black slip are applied with a finger.

2 Pink dots are built up with a slip trailer. Take care that the slip does not run on round surfaces—it may need to dry before you turn the jug to a different angle.

3 Yellow dots over the black dots finish the design. The harder the background slip or clay, the more raised the dots will be.

VARIATIONS

Left: Large platter painted with colored slips, incised, and spotted. JEAN PAUL LANDREAU
Center: Spotted bowl with black slip on white slip, with a honey earthenware glaze. JO CONNELL

Right: Spotted pitcher decorated with black slip on white slip with a honey earthenware glaze. MOLLY ATTRILL

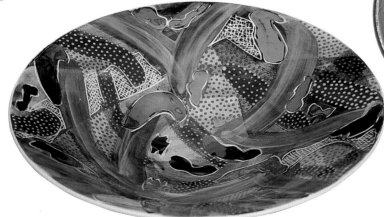

Spraying

SPRAYING COMES INTO ITS OWN when pouring or dipping would be unsuitable, and can produce some delicate effects. Spraying is the method to choose when applying slip to a large, fragile, or complex object; when you have too little slip to pour or dip; or when only a thin coating is needed. It is also a useful aid to decorative effects.

YOU WILL NEED

Spray booth and gun
Prepared colored slips
Leatherhard work to decorate

TIPS

• Clay to be sprayed must be on the dry side of leatherhard. If it is too wet, it will not absorb the slip.

• Do not continue spraying too long. If the build-up of slip becomes too wet, runs will form.

• Slip to be sprayed must be well sieved and not too thick, or it will block the spray gun.

SPRAYING GRADATIONS

1 Spray a leatherhard plate with three differently colored slips, creating a soft blending of one color to the next instead of a hard-edged overlap. Spraying is the only way to achieve this effect.

2 The colored slips need to be built up carefully so that no runs can form. If necessary, pause to allow the slip to dry a little before proceeding, rather than risk the whole piece becoming too wet.

↑ The finished piece by John Commane. The colors of the slips are enriched by a clear earthenware glaze. Underglaze colors as well as slips can also be applied by spraying onto the leatherhard clay.

63

STENCIL WITH SPRAYED SLIP

1 Dampen a thin paper stencil and apply it to the surface of a leatherhard plate. Place the plate in a spray booth.

2 Gently spray the plate with white slip, being careful not to lift the stencil as you do so.

3 Allow the plate to dry until the stencil begins to lift, and then remove it.

Earthenware glazed plate with resist, by John Commane. A translucent green glaze was later applied to this plate. →

Brushwork

can create a flat, opaque coating, brushwork offers more subtle variations of thickness and shading.

It is important to be comfortable with your brush, and there is a vast range to choose from. Slip is heavy, so you need a brush that holds a lot of color, and bristles that are soft rather than stiff. Oriental brushes are especially suitable for a calligraphic approach, and broad ones, known as *hake* brushes, are good for coating a surface. Names such as "scriptliner," "filler," and "shader" give clues to the potential uses of various brushes, but ultimately the brush that works for you is the one to choose.

YOU WILL NEED

Leatherhard piece to decorate

Banding wheel

Slips

Brushes

↑ The finished plate in earthenware. A honey glaze was applied over the slip brushwork to bring out the rich colors.

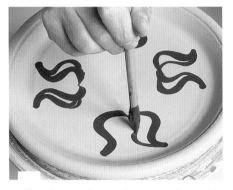

1 A monochrome design is built up with black slip applied with a Chinese calligraphy brush. The brush is very flexible and allows variation in the thickness of line.

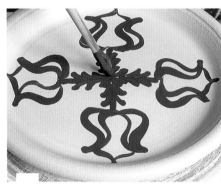

2 The design here is quite formal but because the brush produces loose, flowing lines an individual design is achieved.

3 The brush is very expressive and can be used in a variety of ways. Here the point of the brush is used to make dots.

VARIATIONS

Below and right: *Bowls with slip brushwork. In contrast to the plate above, these two plates are decorated with dramatic bold brushstrokes.*
JONNA BEHRENS

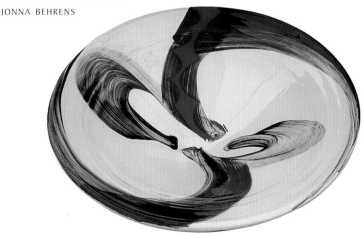

Banding

BANDING IS A GOOD WAY of applying stripes or a flat coat of slip or other color. This example uses a banding wheel: a rotating modeling stand that is usually made of metal. The wheel is rotated by "walking" the fingers around the stem of the wheel, maintaining control with one hand while painting with the other.

YOU WILL NEED

*Leatherhard pot to
   decorate*
Banding wheel
Slips
Wax
Brushes

↑ The banded piece ready for glazing with a honey glaze, then firing. During firing the wax will burn away leaving stripes of contrasting color.

1 Stripes of wax are banded onto a leatherhard cylinder, using a proprietary brush wax, which washes off brushes and is easier to manage than hot wax.

2 A flat hake brush is used to apply a coating of slip over the stripes. The coating is thin and shows the brushmarks.

VERTICAL LINES

In this alternative method, wax is brushed in random vertical lines over an existing coat of yellow slip, and then a layer of darker slip is banded on with a brush.

↑ The finished piece, fired to stoneware 2282°F (1250°C) without a glaze. After biscuit firing, more wax resist was used, with manganese dioxide. Some beads of slip remain on the surface of the wax—a characteristic of the wax resist process.

VARIATION

Below: *Platter made in terra cotta clay and decorated with a banded spiral of wax. White slip was painted over, and after biscuit firing a clear glaze was applied.* JOHN COMMANE

Combing

COMBING IS ANOTHER DIRECT method of decorating that enables the creation of free and fluid marks.

Combing marks are not only made with combs—fingers make good combing tools, and so do objects such as forks, flexible pieces of plastic with notches cut out, and the woodgraining tools used by decorators.

Combing can be done through slip or into the soft clay itself. It is a technique that appears deceptively simple. Effective combing depends on the slip coating being exactly the right consistency—too wet and the slip heals over, too dry and the line is stilted and loses its fluidity. Combed slip varies in thickness and color density, and a carefully chosen glaze can accentuate this effect.

This sequence shows different kinds of combing on a pitcher, through black slip.

YOU WILL NEED

Combing tools of varied types

Leatherhard piece to decorate

Slip

Pitcher

Bucket

1 The pitcher is held in position and slip is poured down one side, then allowed a few moments to drain.

2 A bamboo tool is used to comb a pattern in the slip. This is done quickly, in a sweeping, fluid gesture.

3 Experimenting with different tools is part of the fun. Here, the thumb is used to make interesting marks.

↑ Salt-glazed jug by Alex McErlain, with combed decoration through broad bands of slip.

VARIATIONS

Left: *Salt-glazed stoneware dish, coated with white slip, combed, and stamped.*
JO CONNELL

Center left: *Salt-glazed jug with combed slip decoration under a green ash glaze.* ALEX MCERLAIN

Center: *Salt-glazed pitcher with combed slip decoration.* MICHAEL CASSON

Center right: *Pitcher with clear ash glaze over combed slip.*
WILLI SINGLETON

Far right: *Vase with clear ash glaze over combed slip.* WILLI SINGLETON

WIDE-TOOTHED COMB

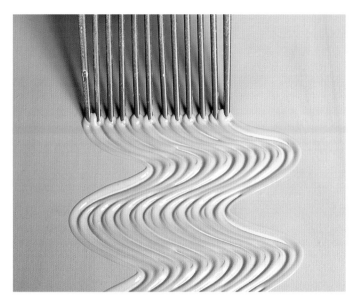

FINGERS

Below, fingers are the only tools used to comb through a layer of very fluid white slip on red clay. It was fired to 1832°F (1000°C) with a clear matte glaze, *see left*.

Above, a wide-toothed comb is used to make fluid marks in a cobalt slip background. The slip was poured on and allowed to dry a little before combing. It was fired to 2282°F (1250°C) with a clear glaze, *see left*.

67

Sgraffito

SGRAFFITO MEANS scratching or drawing into clay—the term derives from the Italian *graffiare*, to draw. Usually, sgraffito is done through an application of surface color to reveal the clay body beneath. The color coating can be slip or other pigment (a mixture of oxide and clay, or oxide and glaze). It can be done with a variety of instruments, from metal loop-ended tools, wooden modeling tools, and skewers, to metal points, needles, and craft-knife blades.

Sgraffito through slip can be done at various stages. Combing (*see page 66*) could be regarded as a form of sgraffito through wet slip, but as the slip dries it is possible to achieve a wealth of effects. When clay and slip coating are still relatively damp, sgraffito tools can dig deeply into the background clay. Some of the background may also be removed, so that the design is left proud. At a later stage, when the piece is almost dry, sharp and accurate lines can be made, as illustrated in this sequence in which a fine and detailed form of sgraffito is applied to a porcelain bowl.

YOU WILL NEED

Sgraffito tools
Banding wheel
Slip
Craft knife or excise knife

↑ There is a huge variety of proprietary sgraffito tools available offering different widths of nib, but it is also possible to adapt any pointed tool to achieve sgraffito effects.

VARIATIONS

Left: *Red earthenware plate with a white slip coating and sgraffito lines drawn through, revealing the clay beneath. After biscuit firing a light wash of underglaze color adds shading to the tea cakes.* CHRISTINE GEDDES

Center left: *Earthenware bowl (24 in/60cm diameter). Terra cotta clay with fine sgraffito lines through a white slip background enriched by the use of coloring oxides.* DOMINIQUE KEELING

Center right: *Square earthenware dish with dipped slips and fine sgraffito lines drawn through.*
FRANCOISE DUFAYARD

Far right: *Terra cotta bowl with sgraffito through white slip, covered with a rich honey earthenware glaze.*
MOLLY ATTRILL

Bottom right: *Potato bakers. Sgraffito farmyard creatures on unglazed terra cotta clay. The white slip background has been removed so that the decoration appears almost in relief.*
MOLLY ATTRILL

A bowl is centered on a banding wheel and an intense black vitreous slip is banded onto the outside (*see page 65*).

2 An excise knife is used to draw fine lines, which cut through the surface color to the clay beneath.

3 The piece is almost complete. When dry, it will be fired to 2336°F (1280°C) without a glaze.

A finished porcelain bowl by Louise Darby, showing the high degree of detail achievable by this method.

PRACTICE RUN

Practicing on a simple tile is a useful way to experiment with sgraffito. Paint a white slip evenly over the surface and leave it until it is dry enough to touch. Use a variety of pointed tools to draw in the slip, and assess the different effects that can be achieved.

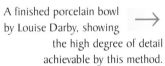

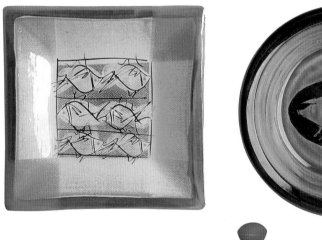

Mocha

A TECHNIQUE DEVELOPED in 19th-century England, mocha derives its name from a quartz known as mocha stone, which bears a mosslike pattern.

This fascinating effect relies on a reaction between a wet surface coating of slip and a mixture of metallic oxide and a special "juice;" here, a concentrated infusion of tobacco and water. The juice—about one cigarette to 3½ fl oz (100ml) water—is boiled for about 10 minutes and then strained. Acids such as vinegar, lemon juice, and wine can be used instead. Potato juice is also successful—but juicing a potato by hand takes some effort!

YOU WILL NEED

Leatherhard clay object (here a tankard)
Light blue slip
White slip
Bucket
Powdered manganese dioxide
Tobacco juice
Slip trailer
Fine paintbrush
Serrated kidney palette

1 A leatherhard red clay tankard is dipped into a large container of light blue slip to approximately half way.

2 White slip is trailed or dotted on top of the blue, and dispersed a little to give a natural "clouds in the sky" effect.

3 While the slip coating is still wet, the pot is held upside down, and a mixture of powdered manganese oxide and tobacco juice is applied at the edge where the slip meets the clay. (Approximately 1 oz/30ml of juice to ½ tsp of manganese dioxide.)

VARIATIONS

Left and center: *Three earthenware pieces by Boscastle Pottery using the mocha technique in different ways, and with imaginative color combinations.*
Right: *The mocha technique can be used with any oxides. Using a white slip background these two tiles were dotted with manganese dioxide (left) and red iron oxide (right).*
Far right: *By feeding the dot with more oxide, and blowing it a little or rocking from side to side, the fernlike pattern can be encouraged to spread and grow. This tile was dotted with cobalt oxide.*

4 As the juice migrates across the slip, it forms minute channels that are filled by the manganese—and a fernlike pattern results. The slip coating must be freshly applied, and the whole process must be done speedily for the mocha effect to succeed.

5 The pattern is repeated around the jug, and the artist adds "fencing" with sgraffito lines (*see page 68*) to further emphasize the landscape effect.

6 A serrated kidney palette is used to create a plowed field, which completes the impression of a winter country scene.

The finished 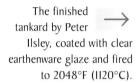 tankard by Peter Ilsley, coated with clear earthenware glaze and fired to 2048°F (1120°C).

TIPS

- Experiment first with small test pieces and different mocha mixtures.
- You will get different results depending on the thickness of the background slip.
- Blow the mocha "fronds" gently to avoid disturbing the background slip. Try using a straw.
- Rocking from side to side or tapping the edge of the tile will encourage the mocha fronds to spread in different directions.
- Allow to dry without disturbance.

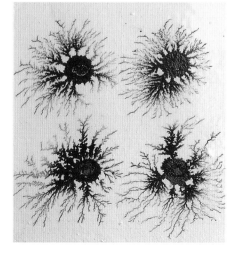

Terra Sigillata

Terra sigillata was the name given to the red gloss pottery made by Roman potters in southern Gaul in the first century. It was later known as Samian ware. The rich gloss is an extremely fine coating of a slip refined by levigation, a technique borrowed from Greek potters whose classical red and black figure vases were made centuries earlier. Contrasting colors resulted from a complex cycle of alternating oxidizing and reducing atmospheres, which indicates astonishing control over the kiln. Slipped areas would turn black under reduction, due to the density of iron oxide, and the body would remain red. Terra sigillata techniques are enjoying a revival today. Amongst studio potters now, however, the term tends to refer to the slip itself rather than the ware from which it originated.

A levigated slip is made by using a deflocculant to keep the finest clay particles in suspension so they can be separated out. The resulting fine-grained slip is applied to a clay surface, then usually burnished and fired up to 1832°F (1000°C).

YOU WILL NEED

Wheel

Brush

Leatherhard pot to decorate

Burnishing tool

Sgraffito tools

Terra sigillata slip as per recipe, right

TO MAKE WHITE TERRA SIGILLATA

9.25 gall (35l) distilled water

3 lb 5 oz (1.5kg) dry white ball clay

25 oz (7.5g) sodium hexametaphosphate*

TO MAKE RED TERRA SIGILLATA

1.5 gall (6l) distilled water

3 lb (1.3kg) fine red clay

1 oz (30g) sodium hexametaphosphate*

some water softeners can be substituted

METHOD

Add the clay to the water, and then put in the sodium hexametaphosphate (which may need grinding in a mortar first). Mix well, and allow to stand for 48 hours. Siphon off the water and discard it, carefully retaining the next layer—about the top third—and discarding the rest.

1 Coat a leatherhard red clay pot with terra sigillata using a soft hake brush. This particular terra sigillata was made from an earthenware clay containing yellow iron oxide. It looks yellow but fires red.

2 When it is touch-dry, burnish it using a piece of thin polythene wrapped around a sponge.

3 Begin to decorate the pot. Carve through the slip with a broad-ended tool using bold "sgraffito" lines.

4 A drill bit is used to form decorative indents in the clay. The potter uses his fingers to support the wall of the pot as pressure is applied.

5 Once decoration is complete the pot will be biscuit fired to 1562°F (850°C). No further firing is necessary. Terra sigillata, which gives an almost waterproof finish, can be applied to biscuit as well as green ware.

↑ The pot is buffed with a wax polish, but would have a pleasant sheen even without it. Red terra sigillata can change color according to the kiln atmosphere, and smoking is often used to achieve a rich, lustrous patina.

Sponge Printing With Slips

Sponging is an interesting way of applying color to clay, allowing the build-up of layers and motifs by printing. Sponges come in all grades. Open natural sponges make pleasing patterns in their own right, but synthetic foam is best for cutting. Dense upholstery foam has a close grain that is easy to manage. It is absorbent enough to hold the slip, and waste ends are readily available. Cutting a sponge is easy if it is moistened and left in the freezer for a while. A sharp knife or scissors will do the job. Curves pose greater problems. A hot needle or wire cuts sponge well, but the resultant fumes can be highly toxic, so extraction must be used. (*See also* Underglaze Printing, *page 85.*)

YOU WILL NEED

Metal kidney
Selection of sponges
Colored slips
Leatherhard piece to decorate

 The finished earthenware bowl, by Jo Connell, fired at 2102°F (1150°C), with clear glaze.

1 This bowl was thrown with care to avoid excessive throwing rings. The surface was scraped with a metal kidney to make it smooth. A range of colored slips was prepared, and sponging begins.

2 The slip needs to be fairly thick, but blot the sponge onto paper after dipping to remove any excess. Here a two-sided sponge is used. Build up colors and patterns.

3 Patterns can be overlapped, provided each coat is allowed to dry before repeated sponging. Dots are applied with a small sponge.

73

ALTERNATIVE METHODS

Here a fairly detailed design is achieved using a sponge cut in the shape of a shell. The sponge was cut with a heated needle, using extraction to take away the fumes. The sponge is dipped into white slip and pressed onto a clay slab.

In this instance a terra cotta slab is printed with a variety of small sponges using a concentrated manganese slip. Masking tape resist adds another dimension to the design.

The slab was formed in a shallow mold and fired straight to 2012°F (1100°C) without the need for a biscuit firing.

Inlaying Slips

THE ANCIENT Japanese art of Mishima—inlaying slips—needs patience and a steady hand, but enables the creation of fine lines of contrasting color, and yields elegant results.

The vessels shown here are slip-cast in porcelain, which gives a smooth white background for this delicate style of decoration. The inspiration for these pieces comes from ikebana—Japanese flower arranging. There is an elegant simplicity to both form and decoration. The slips are also made from porcelain, with the addition of body or slip stains. See the ratios suggested on page 18. These slips are intensely colored.

YOU WILL NEED

*Craft knife or other
    incising tool*
Colored slips
Paintbrush
*Leatherhard piece (here a
    vase)*
Metal kidney palette
Wet and dry emery paper

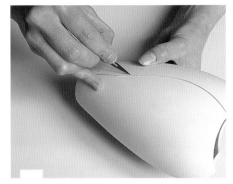

1 Allow the vase to stiffen to a leatherhard consistency, then swiftly incise a flowing line with a knife. Widen the line into a V-shaped groove that is deep enough to hold the slip. This can take time.

Fill the groove **2** with slip until the slip is proud. Compress it slightly to make sure that the groove is full.

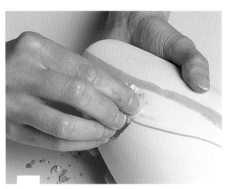

3 Now that the vase and slip have stiffened slightly, the slip can be scraped back with a razor blade to reveal a crisp line that is level with the surface.

VARIATIONS

Left: *Vase made of blue porcelain casting slip, with other colored slips inlaid.* SUE DYER

Center left: *Two porcelain thrown forms. On the left, "Life Spiral Female Form" inlaid with two different slips. On the right, "Life Crystal Male Form" inlaid with three different slips.* CAROLINE WHYMAN

Center right: *Double teapot in thrown and turned porcelain, inlaid with stained porcelain slip when bone dry.* NICHOLAS HOMOKY

Right: *Black porcelain vessel with white inlay.* SUE DYER

Far right: *White porcelain pot with painted slips and inlay.* SUE DYER

4 Continue cleaning up with a sponge, removing all traces of colored slip from the white surface. Even small traces of colored slip will show up badly when fired.

5 After biscuit firing to 1644°F (900°C), rub the work down with emery paper while holding it in a bowl of water, to avoid dust. This gives a final refinement to the surface. The piece is then ready to be fired again, without glaze, to 2265°F (1240°C).

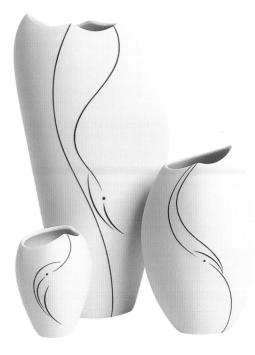

↑ Finished item, by Sue Dyer, with companion pieces.

TESTING INLAID SLIP

1 To check the final color of inlaid slip, it is useful to make an experimental tile. Press a straight edge such as a ruler into a clay slab to form lines. Fill the grooves with different colored slips.

2 When the slip and the body clay have dried to leatherhard, scrape over the surface with a metal kidney to remove the excess. This reveals the colored lines. The tile can be biscuit fired to the required temperature with or without glaze.

Using Resists

THERE ARE MANY WAYS to mask off defined areas so that slip does not contact the clay surface. Thoughtful use of resists allows the build-up of several layers, resulting in an interesting surface decoration with depth. Hot wax is extremely effective and not difficult to use. The best method is to use a double pan, so that the vessel holding the wax does not come into direct contact with the heat but sits in hot water instead. Candlewax or other low-melting wax is suitable, but it must be kept hot. Wax that is too cool tends to set too early and flake off.

Proprietary brush waxes are also available. These do not need heating, and can be washed off brushes. They should be applied thinly and allowed to dry thoroughly (the wax appears milky at first and becomes transparent when dry). Latex is another useful material. It can be purchased from art stores as masking fluid or as latex adhesive, or in larger quantities from sculptors' suppliers. Unlike wax, latex can be peeled off easily once its work is done, or it can stay in place and burn away during firing. Again, it must be allowed to dry before its resistive properties will work.

Newspaper is another useful and inexpensive resist, and one that is far more effective than quality paper. Resourceful potters will find other materials that meet their purposes, and many ways of using resists.

YOU WILL NEED

Wax or paper (florists' wrapping or newsprint)
Colored slips
Sponges
Leatherhard work to decorate
Needle or pointed tool

1 Cut some paper shapes in a stack, about six at a time. Florists' wrapping paper was chosen here because it is thin and flexible but sturdy.

2 Arrange the pieces in the bowl and decide how to fit them into the circular space. This leatherhard dish was made from red clay, but white clay could also be used.

VARIATIONS

Left: *Stoneware glazed vase with leaves applied as resist with slip.*
WILLI SINGLETON
Center left: *Press-molded dish, which has been decorated with poured slip, paper resist, some incising, and a handprint.* JILL FANSHAW KATO
Center right: *Elaborate patchwork pattern created using latex resist with painted and incised slips.*
CHRISTINE GEDDES
Right: *One of a series of salt-glazed stoneware bottles with paper-resisted slips.* JO CONNELL

4 Gently sponge a different-colored slip over the entire surface, covering the leaves while taking care not to dislodge them.

3 Dampen the cutouts, using a water spray or a sponge, and smooth them down to make a contact with the surface.

5 Other leaf shapes are applied to the rim once the first layer is touch dry, then a second layer of slip is sponged on.

6 As soon as that layer is touch dry, the paper dots that form the final layer of the resist pattern are applied. This is followed by the final layer of slip.

7 As the dish dries, the paper begins to lift, and can be removed carefully with a pointed tool or needle.

77

↑ Earthenware dish by Gerry Unsworth, with a clear glaze over paper resist leaf decoration.

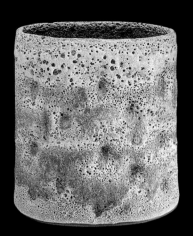

Chapter 2 TECHNIQUES USED AT THE BISCUIT STAGE

Biscuit-fired ceramic is porous, chalky, pale—and unfinished. It demands additional treatment in both tactile and visual terms. There are all kinds of ways to enhance the qualities of biscuit ware, relying on the potter's skill in the use of glaze and color. A huge palette exists to choose from. The diverse qualities of color and glaze fascinated potters for centuries past—and will do so for centuries to come.

UNDERGLAZE COLORS

UNDERGLAZE COLORS, as the term suggests, are intended to be applied beneath the glaze, usually onto biscuit-fired ware. There are many other ways of treating them, and they can, in fact, be used on top of an unfired glaze (*see* Majolica, *page 88*) or without a glaze at all (*see* Unglazed Pigments, *page 96*). They come in a variety of forms:

- As a powder—to be mixed with water or a medium.
- As ready-to-use mixtures.
- As crayons or pencils.

There is a wide palette to choose from, and high-temperature underglaze colors are now widely available. The colors are based on metallic oxides, such as iron, cobalt, and copper, and are commercially treated so that they are stable and consistent. The colors will vary, however, according to a number of factors: the color of the clay body or slip coating beneath, the type of glaze applied over them, the thickness of application, and so on. Metallic oxides can also be used in their own right as underglaze colors, and tend to be stronger.

Application is a skill, and practice is needed. A frequent mistake is to apply the color too thickly, so that the glaze is partially repelled and does not flow evenly across the work. While the color in the tub often represents the fired color, this is not a universal rule so it is wise to pay attention to labeling (some blues appear purple in the tub, for example). Underglaze colors can also be mixed with metallic oxides to increase the palette, but as with all mixing of ceramic color, take

Above: *Underglaze colors come in a variety of forms, including powders, crayons and pencils, and ready-to-use mixtures.*

BASIC TOOLBOX

Underglaze colors: powders, crayons/pencils, or ready-mixed

Suitable biscuit ware

Brushes, sponges

HEALTH AND SAFETY

- Many ceramic materials are potentially toxic and underglaze colors are no exception. They should not be ingested under any circumstances, so no eating, drinking, or smoking in the workshop.

- Dust from underglaze colors should not be inhaled. Always spoon powders out of pots rather than tipping them— and take steps not to create dust at all, wherever possible.

- Fused into or applied underneath a fired glaze they pose no hazard to health, but unglazed they should be treated with caution and pieces that are decorated in this way are not recommended for food use.

Top: *Saltpot with duck and buttercup spoon, and a bottle with jar. Underglaze colors are used beneath a clear earthenware glaze.* ANNA LAMBERT
Center: *Vessel with sprayed underglaze colors beneath a clear stoneware glaze.* ROGER LEWIS
Bottom: *Totem form using oxides, underglaze crayons, and low-firing gold luster glaze.* BRIAN ASHLEY

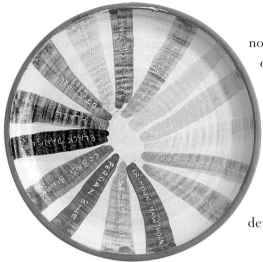

nothing for granted, and make extensive tests. "Know your materials" is one of the key principles to success with ceramics.

Underglaze color has a long history, and one of the classic periods of underglaze painting—with cobalt oxide—was the Chinese Ming dynasty (1368–1644), which is famed for its blue-and-white ceramics. Underglaze decoration is especially durable, since it is protected by a glaze, and is traditionally used in the manufacture of tableware. It can be applied in many ways, including painting, printing, or spraying.

This section demonstrates some of the many ways in which you can develop the art of applying underglaze colors to enhance your work.

Above: Underglaze colors are seen here painted in stripes on top of an unfired earthenware tin glaze and fired to 2102°F (1150°C). This is an example of the majolica technique described on page 88.

Below and right: Platter, and plates, cups, and jug, decorated with sponge printed underglaze colors onto biscuit ware, and coated with a clear glaze. NICHOLAS MOSSE

MIXING UNDERGLAZE COLORS

1 Underglaze colors are available in various forms, including chalks, pencils, and tubes. The ready-mixed type contains a binding agent and ideally should be fired before glazing. Many underglazes are capable of firing to high temperatures, but check with your supplier.

2 It is advisable to always mix up small amounts of colors at a time; large amounts will dry out, and will have to be ground up when hardened. Spoon your colors into a palette, saucer, or glass jar, and keep them apart.

3 Using a slip trailer, gradually add water to the powder color; the trailer gives good control of the amount of water. Ideally, the mixture should be the consistency of thin cream. If it is too thick, it will blister the glaze, if too thin, it will be weak-looking.

Underglaze Painting

PAINTING CAN BE DONE directly onto biscuit ware glazed, in this case, with a clear earthenware glaze. There are many ways of painting, and individual styles will shine through.

It is important to practice strokes with different brushes, because this technique offers a "once only" chance. If mistakes are made, colors can be washed off, but strong pigments can leave a residue. Some colors, such as blues, are much stronger than others, and some colors burn out if thinly applied. As always, it is essential to become familiar with your colors so that you can achieve a balance. Extensive testing repays the effort, because subtle touches of color can make all the difference.

To mix powdered underglaze colors, some potters utilize an underglaze painting medium, usually based on gum arabic. This often means that an additional low-temperature firing is needed to "harden on" the color and burn away the medium, so many people prefer to use just water. Beware, however, of scuffing the decoration, because once applied, it will be very easily damaged.

In the example demonstrated here, the artist takes a bold approach with a very broad brushstroke.

YOU WILL NEED

Biscuit ware to decorate
Underglaze colors
Brushes of various sizes

1 A red clay teapot was coated with cream slip (cream gives a softer, warmer base than white), and was biscuit fired. Now it is held in one hand while the other brushes a bold stroke across the surface. The brush is a worn household paintbrush, and the color is cobalt oxide mixed with water. Here it appears black, but it will fire a rich blue.

2 The second color to be applied is yellow, using a smaller brush at the edges of the blue swathe. Cobalt oxide is a very powerful and dominant color, but, even so, the yellow will add a touch of contrast and will play its part in the final balance of color.

VARIATIONS

Left: *Black-and-white landscape arrows approximately 10 in (25cm) long. Black underglaze, painted, drawn, and sgraffito, under transparent glaze.* PAUL SCOTT
Center left: *"Abstracting Landscape with John Pollex Mug." Porcelain tiled panel. Underglaze painted, sponge printed, and sgraffito under transparent glaze.* PAUL SCOTT
Center right: *Earthenware bowl in the same color scheme as the teapot above and showing equally vibrant and confident brushstrokes.* JAN BUNYAN
Right: *Earthenware soup bowl, red clay with a clear glaze. The decoration uses slips, oxides, and stains as well as sgraffito to produce a rich design with considerable depth.* BENNETT COOPER
Far right: *Earthenware bowl with lively underglaze decoration on buff clay under a clear glaze.* KAREN WOOLF

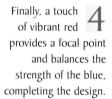

3 Next, the green helps to blend the edges of the cobalt brushstroke. Potters have to become accustomed to working with colors that are not what they seem, and the importance of understanding how colors behave in the kiln is vital.

Teapot by Jan Bunyan, underglaze painted, then coated with a clear earthenware glaze. Fired to 2102°F (1150°C).

Finally, a touch of vibrant red **4** provides a focal point and balances the strength of the blue, completing the design.

83

Underglaze Crayons

MOST ARTISTS WHO USE underglaze crayons combine them with other colors to strengthen their effect, since they are not a strong medium in their own right. They can be interesting when used in conjunction with underglaze colors or oxides. Because the crayons are mixed with clay to form a stick, the fired colors are more akin to slips than the concentrated forms of underglaze, but they give a pleasant sketchlike effect. Some colors are fugitive at higher temperatures and can appear disappointingly weak when fired, so be sure to test the colors first.

Underglaze pencils and crayons can be bought from ceramic suppliers, or you can make your own. When using crayons dust will be created, so you should wear a mask. Colors smudge easily, so avoid touching finished ware until it is glazed.

YOU WILL NEED

Underglaze colors and clay to make your own (see right)

OR ready-made pencils and crayons

Suitable biscuit ware

Brushes

MAKING CRAYONS

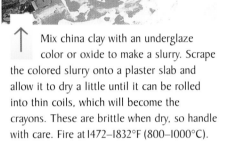

↑ Mix china clay with an underglaze color or oxide to make a slurry. Scrape the colored slurry onto a plaster slab and allow it to dry a little until it can be rolled into thin coils, which will become the crayons. These are brittle when dry, so handle with care. Fire at 1472–1832°F (800–1000°C). Low-fired crayons are soft and smudgy. Fired higher, they become harder and therefore able to make finer lines.

USING CRAYONS

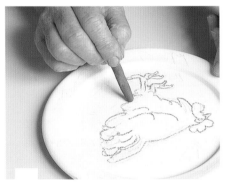

1 After drawing a light pencil outline of the basic image onto the biscuit ware, the first crayon is used.

2 The picture of a chicken is built up with crayons, and background foliage is added in other colors, extending the design over the rim.

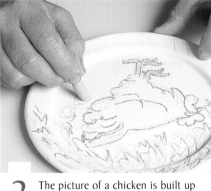

3 Finally a touch of red is applied to the head of the chicken, and a black outline is painted on with a brush. This helps to tie the design together and makes the colors appear stronger.

↑ The finished plate by Jan Bunyan, with clear glaze, fired to 2102°F (1150°C).

COLORS AND QUANTITIES FOR UNDERGLAZE CRAYONS

COLOR	CHINA CLAY	UNDERGLAZE COLOR
Black	3.5 oz (100g)	2.5 oz (70g) Jet Black
Brown	3.5 oz (100g)	2.8 oz (80g) Red Iron Oxide 1.4 oz (40g) Manganese Dioxide
Blue	3.5 oz (100g)	0.4 oz (12g) Cobalt Oxide
Pale blue	3.5 oz (100g)	0.2 oz (6g) Cobalt Oxide
Turquoise, pink, or yellow	3.5 oz (100g)	2.5 oz (70g) Underglaze Color

Underglaze Printing

Underglaze color can be printed onto biscuit ware using a variety of methods. In the ceramics industry, decoration is often applied by screen printing. The studio potter can use this method too, but industrial equipment is needed to print onto ware that is not flat. Biscuit-fired tiles are sometimes available from pottery suppliers or tile stores and can be printed quite easily. The method for direct screen print on tiles using on-glaze color (*see page 137*) can be readily adapted for underglaze color. Underglazes can be printed using rubber or sponge stamps. Rubber stamps can make a very precise print, while sponge printing provides possibilities for more free and fluid images.

YOU WILL NEED

Sponges
Scissors and felt-tip pen
Suitable biscuit ware
Brushes

1 The plate was coated with a white slip and biscuit fired ready for decoration. Marks were drawn on the sponge with a felt-tip pen, and the shapes were cut out. Finally, the colors are chosen and then prepared by mixing with water.

2 Yellow is painted onto the lemon-shaped sponge, and blotted onto paper to avoid excess color.

3 Lime green is added to the sponge and used to overprint the first lemon, creating realistic shading.

4 The leaves are printed in the same way: first green, and then a little cobalt oxide is used to highlight the veins and build up layers.

VARIATIONS

Below: *Resist methods have been used on this mug and serving plate set, as well as sponged and painted underglaze.*
NICHOLAS MOSSE
Right: *Earthenware tiles with a lively underglaze decoration, sponge printed* with underglaze pencil lines added on buff clay under a clear glaze.
LORRAINE RICHARDSON

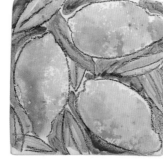

↑ A finished plate by Lorraine Richardson, with clear glaze applied and fired to 2102°F (1150 °C).

DECORATIVE USE OF GLAZE PROPERTIES

WHAT IS GLAZE?

Glaze is essentially a form of glass, which becomes fused to the ceramic surface during firing. Glaze can be shiny or matte, opaque or transparent, smooth or textured, or stained with a whole range of colors— earthy, subtle, or vibrant.

The origins of glaze are said to lie in ancient Egypt around 3000 B.C., when sand impregnated with salt became fused by fire. Silica (sand) is the glass-forming ingredient of glaze. The other two constituents of a basic glaze are aluminum oxide (a stiffening agent) and flux (an agent that causes the mixture to fuse). Color can be added in the form of metallic oxides or ceramic stains, but is present in some raw materials also. The chemistry of glaze is fascinating but complex, and infinite variety can be achieved through study and experiment.

WHY GLAZE CERAMICS?

Glaze can be used for several reasons. It can be supremely functional, strengthening the clay body as it becomes fused to it, making it nonporous, smooth, and hygienic to use. It can also be purely decorative, admired for its rich depth of color or gloss, or sometimes so textured or dry as to render a pot completely nonfunctional. Glazes can be bought ready made, but many potters mix their own, which is a great learning process and also more economical.

BASIC TOOLBOX

Glazes: proprietary or your own (see recipes for materials needed)

Wax (hot or water-based)

Latex

Spray facilities: spray booth with extraction and spraygun (optional)

Underglaze colors and pencils

Brushes and sponges

Tjanting tool

Top: *Thrown platter, tin glazed and decorated with wax resist and cuerda seca techniques along with oxides and underglaze colors.* VICTORIA HUGHES
Center: *Earthenware thrown and altered vessel with sprigging and a chrome/iron glaze.* ASHLEY HOWARD
Bottom: *Thrown, oxidized stoneware pot with a lithium glaze over a silicon carbide slip. The glaze is applied in layers to vary the richness in texture. The glaze reacts with the silicon carbide giving texture, while oxides are added to the glaze to give color.* KATRINA PECHAL

HEALTH AND SAFETY

Sensible precautions should be taken when storing glaze materials. Ensure that clean, sealed, and properly labelled tubs are used. When handling glaze materials, oxides, and colors observe the basic hygiene rules in the Health and Safety section on page 154, and wear a mask to avoid inhaling dust. Wipe up spillages immediately and wash hands frequently. Flint and quartz are particularly troublesome when inhaled and should be stored in dampened form.

METAL-RELEASE TESTS

Some glazes are unsafe for domestic use. Toxic metals may leach out—when they are not completely fused within the glaze, the surplus metal remains soluble.

When formulating glazes for food use it is wise to have them professionally tested by a metal-release test. This test measures the amount of toxic metals released by a glaze into a solution of acetic acid, simulating the effects of using the vessel for wine, vinegar, or fruit juice etc. Above a certain level, the glaze would not be acceptable. Glazes containing compounds of lead, barium, cadmium, selenium or large amounts of copper oxide are especially risky.

Specialist advice should be taken from a glaze chemist or your supplier, if there is any doubt.

TEMPERATURE BANDS

Glazes can be formulated to mature at all temperatures, but for practical purposes, "temperature bands" between about 1652°F and 2462°F (900°C–1350°C) are generally used. The higher the temperature, the harder and more durable the clay and glaze. Four temperature bands frequently referred to in this book are:

Raku	approximately	1652–1922°F	900–1050°C
Earthenware	approximately	1922–2156°F	1050–1180°C
Stoneware	approximately	2192–2372°F	1200–1300°C
Porcelain	approximately	2264–2462°F	1240–1350°C

APPLICATION

This section explores just a few of the effects that glaze can impart to ceramic surfaces, with particular attention to its application. While an attractive glaze can enhance a good pot, it cannot turn an ill-considered form into something beautiful. In fact, glaze application takes practice, and the beginner may be disappointed by runs, drips, and patchiness. Experience will tell how thickly a glaze should be applied for the desired effect: a universal rule is about the thickness of light cream. Application should be as even as possible, and the glaze must be allowed to dry before being touched.

Above: Make test tiles by applying glaze to biscuit-fired tiles, then re-firing them. Firing the tiles in an upright position helps to give an indication of how the glaze will behave on a vertical surface such as the wall of a pot.

Above: Stoneware thrown dish with thick base slip applied, then copper slip applied before barium and lithium glazes. ASHLEY HOWARD

Left: Conkers. Carefully formulated glazes imitate nature perfectly. PENKRIDGE CERAMICS

Above: Thrown white stoneware "boat" glazed with a standard glaze with the additions of titanium, iron, and cobalt. FRAN TRISTRAM

Left: Shino glazed bottle with dry blue ash glaze poured over. Reduction fired in a gas kiln. JOHN JELFS

CHAPTER 7

Majolica

SAID TO HAVE ORIGINATED on the Spanish island of Majorca, majolica was produced throughout the Mediterranean countries from at least the 15th century. Later it flourished in Holland, Italy, France, and England. This "tin-glazed earthenware" became extremely popular in response to a growing demand for whiter, brighter pottery—an interest that was partly sparked by imported Chinese porcelain.

Tin oxide, it was discovered, could opacify a clear earthenware glaze and make it white. It could cover a buff or red clay, so that the color of the clay was often only visible at the foot, where there is generally no glaze. This made it a good imitator of porcelain when demand was at its height. Originally the color was limited to blue (cobalt oxide) on white, but the palette soon expanded to include other colors: iron for brown/rust; manganese for purple; copper for green; and antimony for yellow.

The principle of the majolica technique is to glaze a biscuit-fired piece with a tin glaze before painting it with oxides or underglaze colors—of which there is a wide variety now available. The color is mixed with water or, in some cases, a little of the glaze, and painted directly onto the unfired tin glaze. The painting must be bold and direct, since there is no margin for error. If mistakes are made, the glaze must be washed off and the exercise restarted.

YOU WILL NEED

Biscuit ware to decorate
Earthenware tin glaze
Underglaze colors
Brushes

TIN GLAZE*	
1940–2084°F (1060–1140°C)	
Lead Bisilicate	60
Standard Borax Frit	9
Cornish Stone	15
China Clay	5
Tin Oxide	7
Zirconium Silicate	7
Zinc Oxide	2
Bentonite	2

*After Daphne Carnegie, from an original recipe by Alan Caiger Smith

1 This bowl (made from red clay and biscuit fired) was glazed and allowed to stand for 24 hours before painting. This allows the surface to settle. It would also be possible to fix the surface a little with gum arabic or a glaze binder. Guidelines are drawn lightly with a soft pencil.

VARIATIONS

Left: *Majolica has been applied to stoneware, using red iron and cobalt oxides painted onto the unfired glaze.*
ANDREW MCGARVA
Center left: *Tin-glazed earthenware demonstrating the skilled use of calligraphic brushwork.*
ALAN CAIGER SMITH
Center right: *While majolica is traditionally earthenware, here the technique has been applied to a stoneware glaze.* THUNIG POTTERY
Right: *Brushed-on decoration using oxides and underglaze color, and wax resist techniques on a tin glaze.*
VICTORIA HUGHES
Far right: *Majolica bowl with cobalt oxide and underglaze colors.*
MOLLY ATTRILL

2 Painting begins. The colors are mixed with water, with the addition of a little glaze for the stronger hues.

3 The design is built up using a combination of finely painted lines and broad, free-flowing brushstrokes.

4 The fine lines provide definition for broader areas of soft color, which is applied as a wash, giving a shaded effect. During firing the colors will mellow somewhat, giving the characteristic look typical of this technique.

The finished majolica fruit bowl by Lorraine Richardson, fired to 2102°F (1150°C). →

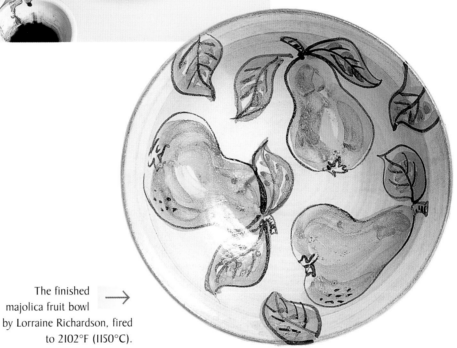

89

Pouring and Dipping Glaze

THESE TECHNIQUES ARE very similar to the methods for pouring and dipping slip (*see pages 56–57*) but there are some additional points to bear in mind. If the work is small enough to be held in one hand, pouring and dipping are excellent methods of applying glaze. A footring is a useful holding device and provides a natural stopping point for the glaze. Glaze should be wiped back a little from the base to allow for any runs, and a footring enables you to do this.

To dip a tall object you will need a deep container of glaze, and if a bowl is not big enough for wider pieces, you may need to improvise with a garbage can or a baby's bathtub. A glazing claw enables a piece to be immersed in the glaze completely when it cannot be conveniently held with the fingers. Any areas not to be coated, such as the base, should first be waxed.

YOU WILL NEED

Substantial amount of glaze in bucket or bowl

Jug

Wax (optional)

Biscuit ware to glaze

Glazing claw (optional)

1 The base of this pot is coated in brush wax to repel the glaze where it is not required. (Glazing the base is only possible if the pot is to be fired on stilts, and these are not commonly used at stoneware temperatures.)

OVERLAPPING EFFECTS

Pouring and dipping can create swathes of colored glazes, including overlap effects. To achieve these, apply each coat as soon as the one beneath is touch dry. If the glaze is too dry, it may bubble or be pulled off by the next layer.

Not all glazes are happy to overlap, and unexpected results can occur—so test first. However, many so-called "faults" become decorative effects in their own right, and overglazing can give interesting results. Similarly, glazes that mature at different temperatures can produce exciting effects.

2 Now that the wax is dry, the pot is dipped sideways into a bowl of glaze which is sufficiently wide and deep to accommodate it.

3 When the glaze is dry enough to touch, the pot is held and dipped the other way, overlapping the first glaze in the middle.

VARIATIONS

Left: *Raku-fired vessel, which was dipped in a white crackle glaze.* GERRY UNSWORTH

Center: *Two vessels dipped in matte stoneware glazes.* JOHN COMMANE

Right top: *Raku-fired vessel with poured glaze decoration.* GERRY UNSWORTH

Right below: *Earthenware vase decorated with poured glaze.* JO CONNELL

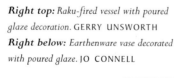

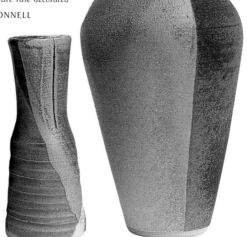

Spraying Glaze

SPRAYING CAN BRING a professional finish to a piece that might be difficult to glaze in other ways. Decorative effects can be achieved by blending one glaze into another, or by spraying a different pigment over or under the glaze. Spraying through a mesh, or deflecting the spray with a piece of cardboard, can create masking patterns. Resists can be attached to the surface, using any material that remains in place long enough to be sprayed—masking tape or pads of damp clay, for example. Beware of using resists that are nonporous, because the glaze may quickly be repelled, causing drips. (*See* Multiple Glazing with Resists, *page 93*, for additional ideas.)

YOU WILL NEED

Spray gun and extraction booth

Glaze

Biscuit ware to decorate

Turntable / banding wheel

TIPS

- Spray from a distance of at least 12 in (30cm) to allow the spray to fan out somewhat.

- Most spray guns have adjustments that allow the spray to vary.

- Clean your spray gun regularly and thoroughly as glaze is abrasive and will wear out the delicate mechanism easily. Always spray clear water through the gun after use to clear it out, and take it apart frequently to check for a build-up of glaze residue.

- A sprayed surface has a tendency to mark easily, so handle with care or preferably do not touch at all until after firing.

1 A white glaze is sprayed over the entire pot. Spraying should be as methodical as possible to ensure even application. It is important that runs don't develop—as soon as the glaze appears wet, move on to the next area.

2 A second glaze (in appearance gray, but actually green) is sprayed over the first. Do not spray too closely to the pot or the application will be too concentrated in one place: 12 in (30cm) is about the right distance, but this depends to some extent on the power of your spray gun and the effect desired.

3 The colored glaze merges from top to bottom—thick to thin. All glazes are likely to appear quite differently according to the thickness of application, and this is a matter for experimentation.

91

VARIATIONS

Left: *Textured bowl with overlapping glazes applied by spraying.*
JOHN COMMANE
Center: *Matte stoneware oxidized glazes were overlapped by spraying on a twisted candlestick.* JO CONNELL
Right: *Jug with sprayed glazes on reduction-fired stoneware.*
FRAN TRISTRAM

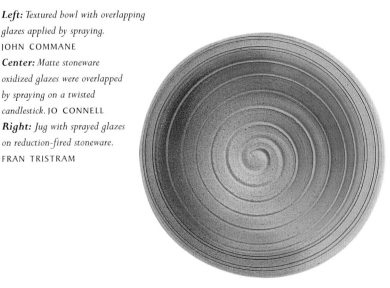

Painting Glazes

APPLYING GLAZE WITH A BRUSH is useful when decorating a single piece with a multitude of colors. The technique is particularly effective for the preparation of tiles.

Although any glaze can be applied in this way, brush-on glazes are manufactured specifically for the purpose. They have an added suspending agent, which gives a thicker consistency than a normal glaze. They come in a wide range of colors and surface qualities, for either raku, earthenware, or stoneware firing temperatures.

The glaze should be applied thickly, so the brush must be well loaded. For a solid color, up to four coats may be necessary, waiting for each coat to dry between applications. A thinner or single coating will result in a more transparent finish. Some specially mixed brush-on glazes work well on dry, unfired clay as well as on biscuit-fired surfaces and on ready-glazed commercial tiles.

CUERDA SECA

The method pictured here is a version of *cuerda seca* ("dry cord" in Spanish). This is an old Moorish technique in which hot wax mixed with manganese dioxide is drawn directly onto tiles, making bold freehand design outlines. It acts as a resist, creating a barrier between the glazes and allowing different colors to be used alongside one another without spreading. It is a very effective technique for outlining and thereby separating the various colors when painting with brush-on glazes, the manganese leaving a dark line as the wax burns away.

YOU WILL NEED

Hot wax

Manganese dioxide

Tjanting tool

Brushes

Brush-on glazes

Industrial- or hand-made biscuit-fired tiles

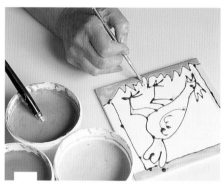

1 Paraffin wax and a little beeswax is melted in a double pan (water is in the bottom part, so that the wax is not in contact with direct heat). A small quantity of manganese dioxide is added.

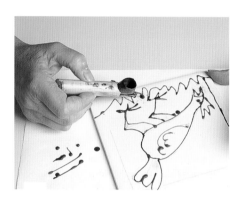

2 A pencil outline is first drawn onto bisque clay or industrial tile. The design is then drawn in wax, using a traditional batik tjanting tool. This has a reservoir to hold the wax, which flows freely out of a narrow tube, acting in a similar way to a slip trailer (*see page 54*).

3 Areas between the outlines are filled with brush-on glaze, using a soft brush. Colors are built up with care to avoid crossing the wax line. Some glazes require several applications, and the manufacturer's advice should be followed.

VARIATIONS

Left: *Jug with a bold pattern in red and green glazes.* CLIVE DAVIES
Right: *Stoneware lidded jar with trailed glaze. Trailing glaze is an effective method of applying one glaze over another.* KAREN ANN WOOD
Below: *Tiles decorated with glaze applied with layers of resist.*
BRONWYN WILLIAMS-ELLIS

↑ Glaze was cleaned away from the edges and the back of the tile and then it was fired to 1976°F (1080°C).

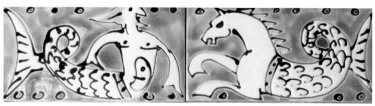

Multiple Glazing With Resists

TWO GLAZES CAN BE OVERLAPPED by various methods to produce a third color, and a resist can be used to protect one part of the work so that glaze does not adhere to it. Wax and latex are often used to repel the glaze. Layer after layer can be built up in this way—with often surprising results. (*See also* Pouring and Dipping Glaze, and Spraying Glaze, *pages 90–91.*)

YOU WILL NEED

Biscuit ware to decorate
Wax
Latex
Needle or pointed tool
Contrasting glazes

The finished oxidized stoneware bowl by John Commane.

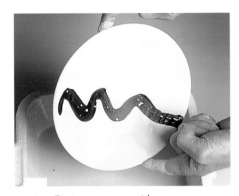

1 First we use wax, with manganese dioxide added. When the wax burns off, the manganese will be left behind as a dark brushmark on the surface of the clay. Both hot wax and brush wax are effective when used in this way. A glaze is poured over and is repelled by the wax resist.

2 Now latex is dribbled on with a pointed tool. It is very liquid, so it can be difficult to apply. However, it has the advantage of being removable, so it will not resist further applications.

3 A second glaze is poured over, and now the latex is removed. A third glaze, not resisted by the latex, could now be applied if desired.

93

VARIATIONS

Left : *Glaze was sprayed and brushed onto this piece, building up colors in variable thicknesses to achieve different intensity of color over latex resist.*
ANDREW MASON
Center: *Vase decorated with glaze over a brushed-on wax resist.*
CAROLINE GENDERS
Bottom right: *Sculptural form using resists and two glazes of differing firing temperatures, giving subtle effects where the glazes interact with each other.* PETER BEARD

Textured Glazes

GLAZE IN ITS NORMAL state can be thought of as clear, shiny, and melted to a glasslike consistency—but textured glazes do not follow these rules. A glaze can be altered in many ways. By studying the chemistry of glazes, we can discover what makes them opaque or clear, matte or shiny, colored or crystalline. So what makes a glaze textured?

In many respects, texture can be considered as a glaze fault. But just as a gardener may see a weed as "a plant in the wrong place," the desirability of texture in a glaze depends upon whether its presence is deliberate. It is certainly not what we would want inside a cup, for example, and it could be unhygienic and unpleasant for food use generally. But texture does have its place, especially in more sculptural ceramics—and here are a few ways of creating it in a stoneware glaze.

Annette Bridges: Pierced sphere with crawl glaze over thin barium glaze, creating a "peeled" effect. The recipes for white crawl glaze and barium glaze appear in the box, right.

CRAWLED GLAZES

Crawling is a fault often caused by applying glaze too thickly, or to a surface that is dusty or greasy. The glaze pulls away into bunches and does not flow properly across the surface. A glaze with high viscosity tends to crawl. A controlled crawl can be created by experimenting with additions of tin or zinc oxide, or zirconium silicate.

A good starting point for experimentation is to add 50 percent zinc, tin, or zirconium to your regular stoneware glaze, and adjust this according to requirements.

RECIPES FOR CRAWLED GLAZES

White crawled glaze
oxidized or reduced 2300°F (1260°C)

Zinc Oxide	50
Nepheline Syenite	50

Yellow/ brown crawled glaze

Tin Oxide	50
Regular Tenmoku Glaze	50

(see recipe in Reduction Firing, page 100)

White crawl glaze 2156°F (1180°C)

Regular Transparent Earthenware Glaze	50
Tin Oxide	50

Barium glaze 2156°F (1180°C)

(Gives a peeling effect when overdipped with the above crawl glaze.)

Nepheline Syenite	50
Barium Carbonate	34
China Clay	16
+ Copper Carbonate (gives turquoise/blue)	3

CRAWLED GLAZES TECHNIQUE

In this example, crawled glazes are painted onto a biscuit-fired bowl to which a black slip was earlier applied.

1 Mark the position of the glazes with penciled lines. Paint on the glazes in layers until you achieve a thickness of approximately ⅛ in (2–4mm). The edges can be overlapped, or mixtures poured or dribbled on, to vary the effects.

2 Just as the glazes do not strictly "fit" the clay during firing, they are also inclined to flake off beforehand and need careful handling. The unfired surface is extremely fragile, and the pot and glaze will separate at the first breath of a breeze. To help adhesion, a binder, such as wallpaper paste or treacle, can be mixed into the glaze.

Bowl with textured glazes by Bridget Aldridge, fired in a reduction atmosphere to 2300°F (1260°C).

VOLCANIC GLAZES

These are crusty glazes with a cratered or lava-like surface. They can be produced by adding silicon carbide to a stoneware glaze. This gives off carbon during firing and causes bubbling. Other combustible materials, such as coarse wood ash, can have a similar effect. A viscous glaze tends to be most successful as a base for volcanic effects, because it is less likely to heal over and become smooth again as the glaze melts.

As a starting point, add 1–5 percent silicon carbide to a stoneware glaze.

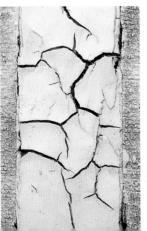

↑ Volcanic glazed candlestick by Paul Young. Glaze was thickly applied—see recipe right, with the addition of 2 percent green glaze stain. As a result of local reduction due to the presence of silicon carbide, the green color has changed to a pinkish brown.

VOLCANIC GLAZE
2282°F (1250°C) *Apply thickly.*

Potash Feldspar	38
Whiting	21
China Clay	21
Flint	11
Titanium Dioxide	6
Talc	3
+ Silicon Carbide	2
(+ color as required)	

CRACKLE GLAZES

Crackle, or crazed, effects are caused by different expansion coefficients between the clay body and the glaze. Low-temperature glazes are often inclined to crackle (*see* Raku Firing: Oxidized, *page 125*). Crackle may develop over a period of time and can be accentuated by soaking in tea, fabric dye, or India ink, or by rubbing a dark oxide into the crackle and re-firing. At high temperatures, crackle can be induced by reducing the silica content of a glaze, or by adding oxides that have a high coefficient of expansion, such as sodium and potassium.

WHITE CRACKLE
2300°F (1260°C) oxidized

Cornish Stone	49
Dolomite	25
China Clay	18
Flint	8

WHITE CRACKLE
2336°F (1280°C) reduced

Apply thickly to produce a large crackle pattern. Rub in India ink to increase the effect.

Potash Feldspar	83
Whiting	9
Flint	8
+ Bentonite	2
(to aid suspension)	

↑ Stoneware bowl by Andrew Matheson, thrown and turned. Reduction fired with a crackle glaze.

VARIATIONS

Left: *Porcelain slip applied to stoneware clay. The high shrinkage rate of the slip has caused it to crack and peel away from the base clay.*

Center: *Copper-stained barium stoneware glaze over a highly textured slip.*
Right: *Stoneware thrown vessel with multiple slip and glaze layers.*
ASHLEY HOWARD

Far right: *Stoneware pot with glaze applied over a silicon carbide slip. The glaze reacts with the slip producing the unusual texture.*
KATRINA PECHAL

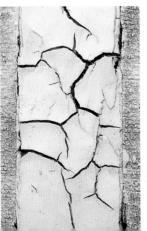
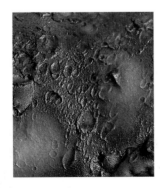

Unglazed Pigments

MANY PIGMENTS can be applied to clay at the raw or biscuit stage and do not need glazing at all. Oxides, underglaze colors, and vitreous slips (known as engobes) make pleasing surface finishes without the need for a glaze—when shine is not required, when the piece is not for food use, or when a glaze covering might spoil delicate detail or texture, for example. At stoneware temperatures of over 2192°F (1200°C), the clay will be vitrified to an extent and nonporous. The clay used here is a white, smooth-textured stoneware containing some fine molochite, and the form is press-molded.

YOU WILL NEED

Leatherhard pot

Banding wheel

Sgraffito tools and a cocktail/barbecue stick

Underglaze colors

Copper carbonate

Dust mask

1 At the leatherhard stage, cut lines into the surface with a sharp tool. Here, a bamboo barbecue stick is used.

WHITE STONEWARE ENGOBE

Flint	10
Potash Feldspar	10
China Clay	10
Ball Clay	5
Nepheline Syenite	5

EARTHENWARE ENGOBE*

China Clay	50
Ball Clay	50
Borax Frit	20

(+ stain to required strength)

*Thanks to Jude Jelfs

2 Cut the modeling clay print into a rectangular shape, wrap it around a suitable former, and secure it with tape.

SLIP GLAZES

Slip glazes, with a high clay content, are part slip and part glaze. They can be applied at the leatherhard or dry stage, and can be fired straight through without an interim biscuit firing. Below are two useful slip glaze recipes:

Metallic satin black
oxidized or reduced 2282°F (1250°C)

Potash Feldspar	40
Red Clay	40
Manganese Dioxide	20

Iron slip glaze
oxidized or reduced 2282°F (1250°C)

Red Clay	45
Borax Frit	30
Nepheline Syenite	10
Talc	10
Red Iron Oxide	5

VARIATIONS

Left: "Two Flat Heads." Press-molded clay colored with stains and oxides. CHRISTY KEENEY

Center left: A variation on the piece created in the demonstration above, using underglaze colors and brush-on glaze. CAROL PEEVOR

Center right: Slab-built boat, decorated with underglaze colors at the leatherhard stage and then biscuit fired. After firing, manganese dioxide is mixed with water and applied thickly, then brushed off when dry, which gives an aged, rusty effect. Fired again to stoneware temperature. SETH DRAPER

Right: Stoneware vessel with manganese dioxide rubbed into textured surface. HANS COPER

Far right: Tiles decorated with underglaze colors. CAROL PEEVOR

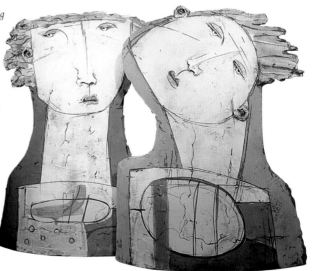

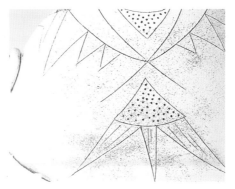

3 When the piece is dry, brush copper carbonate mixed with water across the lines. Brush the dried copper back into the jar with a dry brush or sponge. A dust mask must be worn during this process.

4 The piece is now biscuit fired. Though most of the copper was removed, it clearly remains in the incised lines, appearing at this stage as a khaki color.

5 Apply underglaze colors to the biscuit-fired surface. The ready-mixed colors shown here are easy to apply.

↑ A finished example, by Carol Peevor, uses a combination of underglaze colors and copper carbonate, and in some areas, a brush-on glaze. It was fired to 2282°F (1250°C) in an electric kiln.

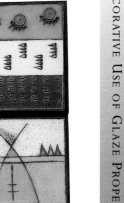

METALLIC OXIDES

Metallic oxides can be applied individually or as mixtures. Here are some recipes for combinations of pigments that give matte results, or a slight sheen, at earthenware or stoneware temperatures:

Bronze
(attractive gold / bronze, but can be runny)

Manganese Dioxide	80
Copper Oxide	20

Black

Red Iron Oxide	40
Manganese Dioxide	20
Cobalt Oxide	10

Rust

Red Iron Oxide	65
Red Clay	35

Brownish blue

Red Clay	92
Cobalt Oxide	8

Dull green

Ball Clay	75
Borax Frit	20
Chromium Dioxide	5

SPECIAL GLAZE FIRINGS

ALL FIRINGS DESCRIBED in the book up to this point could be done in an electric kiln, and the firing procedure for the demonstrations has been a conventional biscuit firing followed by a glaze firing. This by no means has to be the case. The following pages describe processes that deviate from this pattern, or bring another element into the equation. More often than not, the use of special kilns or equipment is involved; these are what make a glaze firing "special."

BASIC TOOLBOX

See individual techniques —for luster, salt and soda, and reduction firings, special kilns are needed.

For crystalline glazes, an electric kiln with a good program controller is advisable.

KILNS

The modern electric kiln is thermally efficient and convenient. In the home or studio, school or college, it is—if used correctly—safe and highly controllable. Often it is the only kind of kiln available, but it offers plenty of scope. For crystalline glaze (*see page 106*), an electric kiln is generally used in conjunction with a sophisticated controller. This regulates the rate of temperature rise and fall (the heating or cooling curve, often known as the "ramp"), or "soaks" the kiln at a required temperature for as long as it is programmed to do so. Such devices have made kiln firing more accurate than it ever was.

Top: Porcelain lidded vessel. Reduction fired, with a rich copper red glaze accentuating a textured surface. JOANNA HOWELLS
Center: Red earthenware bottle, finished with a metallic luster and fired to 1904°F (1040°C). EMILI BIARNES-RABIER
Bottom: Fabric-impressed plate with two layers of glaze. One semi-matte, and four matte glazes overlapping. Reduction fired. JOHN CALVER

Above: This electric kiln has a capacity of 8 cubic feet (0.23m³) and is designed for high temperature use. Elements in the door and floor ensure even firing. There is an automatic damper, pictured here in the open position.

Above: A modern gas kiln, in a down-draft design with an arched roof. Spy holes in the door are arranged so that cones can be viewed in a variety of positions. The burners are fitted with flame-failure devices.

Above: *Mr and Mrs Gourd Jugs. Crystalline glazes using cobalt and copper carbonate for coloring pigments. The tonal change from the top to the bottom of the pots indicates the downward movement of the glaze at top temperature.* KATE MALONE

Above: *This mini salt kiln was designed and made by Steve Harrison, whose work is shown below, left. Made from ceramic fiber, the kiln reaches temperature quickly and can be fired up to stoneware temperature and cooled within a day.*

A gas kiln, obtainable from a pottery supplier, is usually more expensive and less convenient to site and to operate than an electric kiln. But it can do things that an electric kiln cannot—such as reduction firing (explained in detail on page 100) and other techniques described in this section.

Other glaze effects require the kind of kiln that cannot be bought ready-made, and the only way is to build one. Salt and soda firings require a kiln specifically for this purpose (*see page 104*).

To achieve success in the techniques featured in this section, it is necessary to gain a deeper understanding of the glaze chemistry involved, so that the reactions that occur in firing can be interpreted. The problems encountered can be considerable—but the rewards are great. The best way to discover more about your chosen technique is to find an expert practitioner with whom to work, then observe, listen, and learn before going it alone.

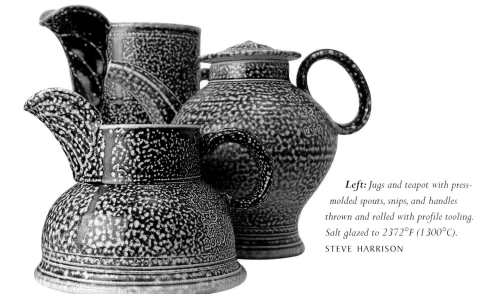

Left: *Jugs and teapot with press-molded spouts, snips, and handles thrown and rolled with profile tooling. Salt glazed to 2372°F (1300°C).* STEVE HARRISON

Above: *This wood-fired kiln is in the process of reduction. Incomplete combustion in a wood-fired kiln, the result of heavy stoking, forces unburnt gases to seek oxygen through gaps in the structure with spectacular results. (See page 100, Reduction Firing.)* STEVE MILLS

Stoneware Reduction Firing

DURING STONEWARE FIRINGS, the atmosphere inside the kiln is either oxidizing or reducing. Electric kiln firing is always mildly oxidizing, and although certain agents can be introduced during the firing to induce a reduction atmosphere, this is likely to shorten the life of the elements. A kiln that burns fuel—usually wood, oil, or gas—is therefore normally used for reduction firing.

In oxidation firing, there is an unrestricted flow of air into the combustion chamber, so the fuel is fully burned. In reduction firing, the air intake is restricted and so some fuel remains unburned. The result of this inefficient combustion is carbon monoxide. This unstable gas takes available oxygen from metals in the clay and glaze in order to achieve the stable form, carbon dioxide. How does this affect pots in the kiln? The oxides most affected are iron and copper. The low oxygen (reduced) forms of iron and copper oxides display different colors from those produced by an oxidized firing.

The photographs below and right illustrate both oxidized and reduced versions of three traditional Chinese glazes and show the effects of a change in kiln atmosphere.

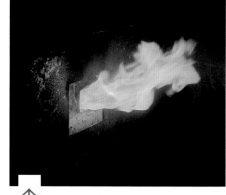

A gas kiln firing at approximately 1742°F (950°C). The front bung (an opening of 2 x 2 in/5 x 5cm) has been removed from this kiln to show how a flame will leap out and grab oxygen from any possible source while the kiln is reducing. (*Photo courtesy of Andrew Matheson.*)

TENMOKU

Tenmoku is an ancient Chinese glaze, though its name was given by Japanese monks. The monks visited monasteries in the Tianmu mountains of China and took the brown glazed bowls back with them to Japan, where the word Tianmu was pronounced "Tenmoku." The glaze contains a large amount of iron, which becomes richer, darker, and more metallic in reduction. One of its characteristics is the "breaking" to a different color where the glaze encounters texture, such as throwing rings.

TENMOKU GLAZE	
Reduced stoneware 2282°F (1250°C)	
Feldspar	40
Quartz	20
Whiting	15
China Clay	10
Red Iron Oxide	10
Ball Clay	5

Two Tenmoku-glazed mugs showing a difference in color due to firing: the mug on the left was oxidized; the mug on the right was reduced. JO CONNELL

VARIATIONS

Left: *Detail of reduced dark celadon bowl with dots of iron slip.* ANDREW HEMUS
Right: *Tenmoku reduced glaze teapot with slips beneath.* DEREK EMMS

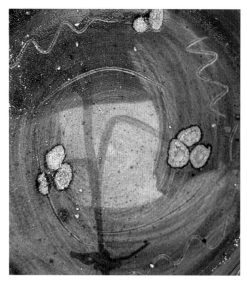

CELADON

Celadon is another glaze of Chinese origin, named for a character in French theater who wore a gray-green costume. It is a feldspathic glaze (a glaze with a high proportion of feldspar) colored with a small amount of iron. It can range from pale turquoise to dark gray-green or khaki, depending on the amount of reduction during the firing and the kind of clay body used. In oxidized conditions, a celadon glaze will appear more yellowish, as shown on the pitchers, right.

A CELADON GLAZE	
Feldspar	68
Whiting	12
Flint	10
Ball Clay	8
Red Iron Oxide	2

↑ Two pitchers, both showing celadon glazes on porcelain: reduced on the left and oxidized on the right. JOANNA HOWELLS

COPPER RED

Copper is the oxide that can give the most dramatic effects under reduction.

A small amount of copper can give a deep blood red in reduction. In an oxidized firing, it will be pale green. Illustrated below are two pots by Mike Reynolds glazed with a copper red that show the remarkable difference between oxidation and reduction. The pot on the left is oxidized stoneware; the one on the right is reduced.

Copper red glazes were first developed in Sung dynasty China (A.D. 960–1279). As legend has it, the glaze arose by accident in a Chinese climbing kiln into which a pig had foolishly strayed. A climbing kiln is built on a hillside, and consists of a number of chambers. These kilns can be very large and a pig would have no trouble walking in! Most of the pots from this firing were uninteresting but one shone out a rich, deep red. The potter sent this one to the emperor, who ordered more. The potter was unable to oblige, since he had no idea why the color had occurred in the first place. In desperation, after several unsuccessful firings, he threw himself into the kiln, whereupon all the pots turned a beautiful deep red! The burning body had brought about a reduction atmosphere which—too late for the potter—had achieved the desired effect.

These days, production methods are mercifully less drastic. Copper reds do, however, require much patience and practice. Reduction should begin relatively early in the firing and must proceed rapidly to a high stoneware temperature (approximately 2336°F/1280°C). The glaze must be thickly applied and is very fluid, so it can easily run down the pot. Different reds can be achieved according to the glaze constituents and firing methods. Two copper red recipes are given here.

↑ Two pots with copper red glaze illustrate the difference between oxidation (left) and reduction (right). MIKE REYNOLDS

COPPER RED I	
Feldspar	36
Whiting	24
China Clay	12
Ball Clay	12
Flint	12
Tin Oxide	6
Copper Carbonate	0.25

COPPER RED 2	
Feldspar	40
Whiting	20
China Clay	10
Quartz	30
Talc	5
Copper Carbonate	0.5

In in-glaze luster and raku firing (see pages 102 and 120), reduction is used in a different way: the clay and glazes are deprived of oxygen after the glaze is fired to maturity but while it is still molten. In smoke firing (see page 110), carbonization is the result of local reduction, as oxygen becomes used up in the fuel combustion process.

A TYPICAL STONEWARE REDUCTION FIRING CYCLE

The kiln is taken up to 1652°F (900°C) at approximately 302°F (150°C) per hour or higher, then reducing begins. This is normally done by pushing in the chimney brick part-way and reducing the air intake. During reduction the temperature will not rise as rapidly, due to inefficient burning of fuel. Most potters like to alternate reduction and oxidation until the temperature reaches the desired peak (2282–2372°F/ 1250–1300°C), and to end with an oxidizing "clean-up" to make sure that top temperature is reached. The air inlets are then closed and the kiln allowed to cool naturally.

If the bung at the front of the kiln is removed while the kiln is reducing, a flame often leaps out seeking to grab oxygen.

Reduction firing lends warmth to the clay itself, especially to bodies containing iron. This coil-built vase by Jill Fanshawe Kato illustrates the "toasted" quality of reduction-fired clay. Coil-built, paper resist, and painted slips; reduction fired to 2318°F (1270°C).

Luster Reduction Firing

WE REFER HERE TO traditional and in-glaze luster techniques—not to be confused with oxidized lusters (*see page 140*). Luster decoration is produced by a thin metallic film on the surface of a glaze. This ancient technique was brought to perfection by Persian potters and was later carried to Spain, from whence it spread to other parts of Europe. Different methods are utilized and developed in personal ways through experimentation. Perseverance is necessary to achieve success, because the chemistry involved is complex. Luster firing can, however, be extremely rewarding, and sometimes becomes compulsive!

Two methods of achieving luster are described here. The clay-paste, on-glaze technique, which offers scope for sharper and more linear decoration, and the in-glaze method, which gives bolder effects, because of its greater integrality.

In the on-glaze "clay paste" method, the biscuit-fired work is coated in a soft tin glaze and fired at 1742–2030°F (950–1110°C). Then salts of copper and silver are mixed with a clay paste and applied to the surface of the fired piece. The piece is given another (third) firing to about 1256°F (680°C), in a reduction atmosphere. During this, the glaze melts again—just enough to respond to the changing atmosphere—and the copper and silver in the paste form a thin luster layer in the upper surface of the glaze. After firing, the blackened paste is removed and a brilliant luster is revealed beneath. Wood firing is the traditional and preferred method.

When using the post-firing reduction in-glaze method, the two important elements, silver and copper, are mixed into the glaze itself or painted onto the unfired glaze. Only one glaze firing is therefore necessary. As the kiln cools, a reduction atmosphere is introduced causing a chemical reaction. Volatile elements within the glaze bring the reduced copper and silver to the surface and they are turned into a thin reflective film of metal. Firing is usually done in a wood- or gas-fired kiln, but an electric kiln can be used with a gas torch introduced for a short time on cooling to produce a reduction atmosphere. Under reduction, copper gives red tones, silver nitrate gives ivory to yellow, bismuth gives iridescent effects, and cobalt gives blue. This method is frequently done at low earthenware temperatures, but the sequence on these pages demonstrates a high-temperature method.

Luster kiln, showing (left to right): The damper in the flue (chimney), which can be adjusted to vary the degree of reduction; the gas burners, mounted on a metal frame for safety and convenience; the pyrometer, indicating the temperature in the kiln. A digital pyrometer is used for preference, as it provides greater accuracy.

HIGH-TEMPERATURE LUSTER

This in-glaze, high-temperature luster technique makes use of the reducing atmosphere in the cooling kiln. The atmosphere, starved of oxygen, seizes it from metal oxides within the glaze. The high-temperature firing schedule reduces the copper oxide in the glaze, resulting in a deep red. A thin metallic film is caught at the surface, and lustrous effects with purple, gold, and pink are possible.

1 A thick layer of glaze is applied to achieve the best effect, which begins to occur as the glaze moves into its molten state. To control the glaze movement, these pieces have restricted areas of glaze, poured over patterns created by wax resist. Slips are applied to the body before biscuit firing. The glaze used here contains an unusually high percentage of copper carbonate, giving a dense red luster.

VARIATIONS

Left: Clay paste silver luster over a cobalt and chrome underglaze. Decoration was applied with a brush and small sponge, and the piece was reduction fired. JONATHAN CHISWELL JONES
Center: Oyster dish with clay paste luster. PAUL SPENCE
Right: Grebe Displaying. Stoneware with smoked copper luster, from the firing demonstrated above. JANET HAMER

2 Kiln packing: Bird sculptures are placed in a top-loading kiln, on the base shelf and a smaller shelf above. A pyrometer probe registers the temperature—timing is crucial, and a digital pyrometer immediately shows any rise or fall. The kiln chamber is built with walls of firebrick lined with ceramic fiber. The lid consists of fiber blocks on a framework.

3 The chamber is heated by one propane gas burner and is fired to 2228°F (1220°C) in an oxidizing atmosphere. Then the burner is turned off, and the kiln is clammed up (air inlets are closed to stop additional intake of oxygen). The kiln cools quickly, and at 1778°F (970°C) sticks of wood are introduced through the burner port. These char beneath the base shelf, creating a reducing, smoky atmosphere. The process is repeated six or seven times.

4 Fired pieces show glints of red and luster. Sometimes a black residue must be cleaned off in order to reveal the dramatic glaze qualities.

(*Photos by Janet Hamer.*)

Swimming Drake by Janet Hamer in smoked copper luster stoneware, 12 in (31cm) high.

COPPER RED LUSTER GLAZE

Janet Hamer, who demonstrates luster reduction firing, above, uses the following recipe for her copper-red luster glaze.

Potash Feldspar	19
Lead Bisilicate	19
Standard Borax Frit	19
Whiting	18
Flint	16
China Clay	8
Bentonite	1
+ Copper Carbonate	4

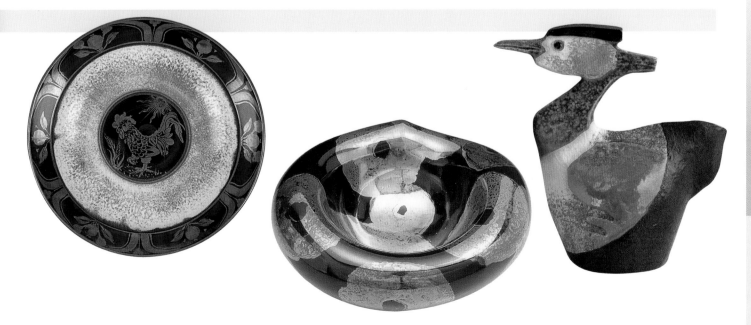

Salt and Soda

BOTH SALT AND SODA can bring a distinctive "orange-peel" quality to the surface of vapor glaze. During the firing, salt or soda is introduced into the hot kiln. The sodium reacts with the silica and alumina in the clay to produce the colorless glaze sodium aluminosilicate. The surface texture comes from the relative coarseness of the silica particles in the clay. These attract the formation of the glaze in an uneven way to produce the beadlike, mottled, orange-peel effect, sometimes referred to as a "tiger-skin" surface. Any color comes from the oxides in the clay and from the application of colors in the making and decoration stages.

SPECIAL KILNS

Salt and soda firings must be carried out in kilns specially designed for them, because the vapor component has a detrimental effect on the internal structure of the kiln. Kilns can be fired with gas, oil, or wood, but must not be electric. Both salt and soda kilns should be located outdoors. Depending on how the salt is introduced, salt firings can produce a considerable plume of unneighborly dense mist during the salting and should not be sited in an urban area. The use of soda avoids the mist but any vapor fumes are considered undesirable in a built-up area.

↑ This soda kiln is built from heavy, high-alumina firebricks. Firing begins on a low heat overnight and is steadily increased the next morning. The soda is introduced in the early evening, and the firing is finished around 10 o'clock, a total of around 27 hours.

DECORATIVE VARIATIONS

The usual way of adding color is with slips containing various proportions of coloring oxides. Slip can be applied by any of the methods described in earlier chapters and can cover all or part of the piece. Salt and soda firings lend variation to the surfaces of each piece, depending on its position in the kiln and the way the vapor moves around the stacks of pots.

Certain other decorative techniques are especially suitable for salt glaze. Sprigging and embossed decoration, rouletting, and any simple texturing are all effective, because the vapor glaze can be extremely thin and will pick out the finest detail.

Many potters place each of the pots on wadding (small balls of a mix of high-alumina paste) in order to prevent them from sticking to the kiln shelves.

104

VARIATIONS

Left: Large dish with dramatic color effects produced by a combination of slips and salt firing. ROSEMARY COCHRANE
Center left: Jug glazed with a blue slip. This strong form is enhanced by a tactile surface characteristic of salt glaze. WALTER KEELER
Center right: Vase with feather detail has been soda fired to produce a mottled effect in parts. MAY LING BEADSMOORE
Right: Detail of decorative handles on salt-fired bowls. ROSEMARY COCHRANE

Far right, top: Impressed details and surface texture on these spoons and spoon rests accentuate the unique character of each soda-fired piece. MAY LING BEADSMOORE
Far right, bottom: Soda vapors are not distributed around the kiln as readily as salt. The results can be patchier, adding a flashing to heavily glazed areas. LISA HAMMOND

2 Packing the kiln. The vapor will create a glaze on all surfaces, and all of the kiln furniture must be coated with a resist. The doorway is bricked up with firebricks, leaving a spyhole.

3 The salt is introduced into the kiln over an extended period of time during the height of the firing, around 2300°F (1260°C). Here, damp salt is loaded onto a piece of angle iron and tipped into the firebox. Some potters spray dry salt into the kiln. Spraying a saturated solution is the preferred method for introducing soda, and can also be used for salt.

4 During the salting period, trial rings are drawn from the spyholes to judge the progress of the glazing.

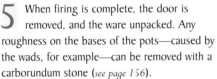

5 When firing is complete, the door is removed, and the ware unpacked. Any roughness on the bases of the pots—caused by the wads, for example—can be removed with a carborundum stone (*see page 156*).

↑ Lidded pot by Rosemary Cochrane. The use of brushed slip decoration is enhanced by the variable orange-peel effect of the salt glaze.

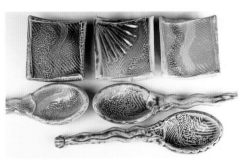

Crystalline Glazes

UNDER CERTAIN CIRCUMSTANCES, crystals form within a glaze as it cools—a process that was noted and developed by the large ceramics factories of Europe in the 1850s. Crystalline glazes can be either microcrystalline or macrocrystalline. Microcrystalline glazes have small crystals, which can be seen suspended below the surface of the glaze. Glazes with these small crystals are often referred to as aventurine glazes, because of their resemblance to aventurine quartz. A macrocrystalline glaze is one that shows large, well-developed crystals, sufficient to produce a decorative effect. Zinc, calcium, barium, and titanium tend to cause crystals. Rutile and ilmenite are also useful.

MACROCRYSTALLINE GLAZES

Crystalline glazes need a pure white and smooth body so that no inherent impurities or surface coarseness can create seeding for the crystals and spoil the finished piece. Porcelain is therefore the traditionally preferred body, although a smooth white stoneware can be almost as successful.

Any method of manufacture can be used in the creation of pots for crystalline glazes, provided the surface is smoothed off, either when it is bone dry, or with carborundum paper after biscuit firing. Uncomplicated forms, such as bottles and bowls, are especially suitable.

USING A "CATCHER"

To allow the crystals to grow, the glazes must be very fluid. For this reason, pots are fired on a customized ring-shaped holder known as a "catcher." The center of the ring is the same diameter as the footring of the pot, and an outer trough catches the molten glaze as it runs off the bottom of the pot.

Correct application of the glaze is essential. The bulk of the glaze must be applied to the top third of the piece; the thickness here can be up to $\frac{1}{8}$ in (2mm). When the pots are taken from the kiln, the catcher must be removed from the footring. This is done by applying the flame from a needle-flame blow lamp just below the joint—and expansion does the rest. The sharp edge of the glaze on the footring is then ground with an angle grinder or carborundum stone.

THE FIRING SCHEDULE

Firing crystalline glazes requires an oxidizing atmosphere, because reduction inhibits the crystal growth. A programmed electric kiln is the best choice, because the schedule is fairly complex. The peak firing temperature is between 2300°F and 2372°F (1260–1300°C)—the final 392°F (200°C) being completed rapidly in order to make the glaze fluid as quickly as possible. Having attained its peak, the temperature is reduced as fast as possible by 392°F (200°C). This takes it down to the crystal growth band, which is between approximately 2012°F and 1787°F (1100–975°C). The pots are soaked within this temperature band for three to eight hours to allow crystals to grow and develop in the glassy matrix.

CRYSTALLINE GLAZE for oxidized firing at 2300°F (1260°C)	
Ferro Frit 3110	44
Calcined Zinc Oxide	27
Flint	21
Titanium Dioxide	8
+ Calcined Alumina	0.5
+ Molochite	0.5
+ Finnfix*	0.2

*A glaze adhesive/hardener; gum arabic or gum tragacanth can be used instead. This glaze will produce white crystals on a white background. The real joy starts when coloring oxides are added. Best results generally come from using two or even three oxides or carbonates in the same glaze. Below are some suggestions for additions of oxides:

Apple-green crystals on a white background:
Add: 2% Copper Carbonate
1% Manganese Dioxide

Prussian blue crystals on a tan background:
Add: 0.2% Cobalt Carbonate
0.5% Copper Carbonate
0.5% Nickel Oxide

Violet crystals on a gray background:
Add: 0.5% Cobalt Carbonate
2% Manganese Dioxide

Turquoise crystals on a tan background:
Add: 0.5% Copper Carbonate
0.5% Nickel Oxide
0.5% Red Iron Oxide

Gold crystals on a green ground:
Add: 2% Copper Carbonate
3% Manganese Dioxide

Ivory crystals on a white background:
Add: 1.5% Red Iron Oxide

A post-firing reduction can be done on glazes containing copper to create bright copper luster crystals (see Luster Firing, page 140). Select finished pots from the oxidation firing and place them in a gas-fired kiln. Take the temperature up to 1517°F (825°C). A reducing atmosphere is induced while the temperature drops to 1022°F (550°C) over a 90-minute period. Allow the kiln to cool naturally.

1 Throw a "catcher" on which to fire the crystalline-glazed piece—in this case, a bottle. This should then be biscuit fired.

2 Apply a thick layer of glaze with a brush. Concentrate on the top of the form, because the glaze will run down.

3 Stand the bottle on the catcher ready for firing.

4 The fired piece is joined to the catcher due to the fluid nature of the glaze. Detach it with the aid of a needle-flame blow torch.

5 Grind the sharp edges off the base of the piece, using an angle grinder.

Macrocrystalline glazed bottle by Peter Ilsley. Peter believes that good crystalline glazes depend on the successful combination of a trinity of factors: glaze formulation, glaze application, and firing schedule.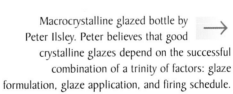

VARIATIONS

Left and right: Details of pots decorated with crystalline glazes, which were painted on by hand. A complex cycle of firing and cooling causes the crystals to grow. KATE MALONE
Below: Macrocrystalline glazed bowl. PETER ILSLEY

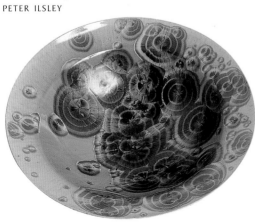

Chapter 3 ALTERNATIVE FIRING TECHNIQUES

It is often said that potters are either mud or fire people—this chapter is for the latter! There can be no better way to understand the action of fire on clay than to participate in smoke or raku firing. From carbonizing to pit firing, the potter interacts with fire throughout—and results range from soft and subtle to dramatically colorful. Pots made this way are truly touched by fire.

SMOKE FIRING

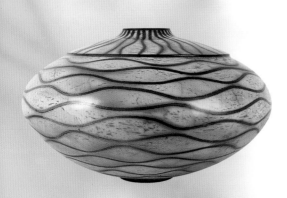

In times past, a certain amount of smoke during firing was unavoidable. Any kiln using combustible material, such as wood, plant material, or dried dung, would inevitably produce smoke. Some early firings were simply bonfires—the pots taking their chance in the flames, with little protection. Early civilizations soon learned the importance of heating pots slowly, and of insulating the fire to keep it burning for longer, giving the best chance of raising the temperature as high as possible. Shards were placed over the bonfire, insulated with mud and dung, and a draft was established beneath the fire.

Independently, in different parts of the world, efficient kilns were developed, and the bonfires became a minority method of firing. Although many cultures still use open firing, studio potters in the Western world have adopted "smoke firing" specifically for the effects of smoke and flame on the surface of their pots.

WHAT IS SMOKE FIRING?

This section describes different methods of firing, but the common factor is that the burning fuel is in direct contact with the pots. Carbon produced in this way is absorbed by the porous body of the pot, which is usually biscuit fired in advance. The resulting colors range from black to brown and gray—sometimes enhanced into more exotic hues by additions of oxides and sulfates, or by using slips before biscuit firing. Smoke firing is usually a low-temperature technique and, unless glazed, the pots remain porous, so they are regarded as nonfunctional. The effects of smoke on pots begins well below that of most "conventional" firings, and most of the

BASIC TOOLBOX

Kilns or metal containers

Sawdust and paper, combustible materials

(Also see individual techniques)

FUELS FOR SMOKE FIRING

- Sawdust and shavings
- Hay, straw, dried plant material
- Shredded paper or newspaper
- Dried dung

Top: *Smoke-patterned pot using tape and clay slip resists. The pot was burnished, biscuit fired, then patterned with the cut masking tape. The area between the tape is infilled with clay slip. Smoke firing burns away the tape but does not penetrate the clay body.* GEOFF TOWNSEND

Center: *Porcelain and "T" material bowl coil-built from a molded base section and burnished. Smoke fired with a slip-resist decoration.* JAQUI ATKIN

Bottom: *Pit-fired pot that was first burnished and biscuit fired to 1922°F (1050°C).* ARDINE SPITTERS

Right: *Chalices and spade vases carbonized using sawdust as fuel. These slab-built forms are treated with under-glaze colors and are glazed inside before smoking.* TESSA WOLFE MURRAY

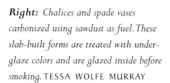

techniques described are, strictly speaking, finishing rather than firing methods. An exception—and there are always plenty in ceramics!—is high-temperature saggar firing (*see page 114*).

HOW DOES SMOKE FIRING DIFFER FROM RAKU ?

There are no hard and fast rules here, especially since the term *raku* is now used in such a diverse way. Generally speaking, however, raku is fired at a higher temperature (around 1832°F/1000°C) than smoke firing, which works from temperatures as low as 752°F (400°C). In post-reduction raku firing, pots are already very hot when they come into contact with combustible material, whereas in smoke firing the pots are started off cold—or possibly preheated just to minimize thermal shock. In smoke firing, the action of smoking occurs during firing; in raku it occurs after. The technique of slip resist (*see page 76*) covers methods used in both smoke firing and raku—the major difference being that of temperature.

Above: *Vessel made from porcelain and stoneware clays, mixed with a large amount of grog. Such pots are burnished and biscuit fired to 1922°F (1050°C) before being pit fired. Slate has been added as decoration.* ARDINE SPITTERS

IMMEDIATE RESULTS

All types of ceramic firing have their own particular fascination. Some processes, such as crystalline glazes (*see page 106*), take many hours of programmed temperature control, and with experience, give a relatively consistent result. Others, such as salt and soda firing (*see page 104*), require hours of input by the potter—adjusting reduction atmosphere, introducing salt, even building the kiln in the first place. Smoke firing, by contrast, can give a surface finish almost instantly, with minimal equipment and expense—but always with a degree of unpredictability. The immediacy of the process, coupled with anticipation of the results, brings a special excitement to the firing process.

Subtle marks often reflect the action and character of flames, and seem to follow the form naturally. Smoke firing appeals to the "pyromaniac" tendencies of potters and provides an exciting diversion from the predictable nature of electric-kiln firing. Today, however, we have the best of both worlds—and breakages can be minimized by biscuit firing the pots first, taking them slowly through that critical phase when moisture is driven from the clay. With practice, smoke firing can become less of a lottery, but it will never be totally predictable. The process can also be achieved using very little smoke: with care, it can be done in an environmentally friendly manner with no inconvenience to neighbors.

Far left: *Two tall bottles, thrown, turned, and burnished. Copper luster is fired directly onto the burnished surface to emphasize certain areas of a piece, which is then finally fired in a saggar in the kiln. Wax polish is applied to seal and shine the finished work.* CHRISTINE GITTINS

Left: *Pit-fired porcelain vessel. See page 112–113 for a description of the firing method.* ELIZABETH MICHL

Pit Firing

FIRING IN A PIT CAN BE QUITE efficient since there is good insulation from the walls of the pit, which has no gaps to allow air in. A pit can be any size, but if too shallow then oxidation will be excessive; too deep and it will be difficult to pack. An optimum depth would be around two feet (60cm). Shallower than that, it may burn too quickly. Fuel is usually a mixture of fast and slow burning types, so that combustion is maintained throughout the firing and a reduction atmosphere is created around the pots. Pots are often treated with slips and oxides to encourage colors—iron together with salt can give orange, copper carbonate gives reds and soft pastel pinks. Seaweed, fruit and vegetable peelings, and other plant material are sometimes used as fuel. Chemical reactions occur during combustion and all these affect the finished surface in various ways. The pots remain porous when fired.

THE FIRING PROCESS

The control of fire in a large hole in the ground for eight hours, placing the pots, the oneness of earth and fire giving results like no other…it is emotional and exhausting! It may seem like luck when beautiful pots emerge from this inferno, but this is definitely not the case. A lot of careful preparation and attention to detail is required.

Pit-fired porcelain vessel by Elizabeth Michl, thrown and previously biscuit fired. Colored with copper carbonate.

Pots waiting to be packed in the pit, which has sawdust in the bottom and is lined with timber. The pots are made from white stoneware clay and coated with terra sigillata before biscuit firing in an electric kiln to 1922°F (1050°C).

VARIATIONS

Left: Pots are made from white stoneware clay and coated with terra sigillata type slip before biscuit firing. A solution of copper carbonate is sprayed onto the pots, then they are pit fired with salt, seaweed, and more copper carbonate. See demonstration above. ELIZABETH MICHL

Center: Two vessels made from a mixture of porcelain and stoneware clays, with added grog. Burnished and biscuit fired to 1922°F (1050°C), then treated with sulfates. The pit kiln is filled with a mixture of wood and sawdust and burns slowly for 48 hours. ARDINE SPITTERS

Right: These pots are thrown in sections and pieced together, then burnished, before firing to 1562°F (850°C) in an electric kiln. The pit kiln is then prepared with a layer of sawdust in the base and

the pots are arranged on this before covering with the rest of the fuel. The pit burns for three days and is left to cool, then the pots are taken out and polished with wax. TAMASINE HOLMAN

2 Stacking the pit with pots and wood. Copper carbonate, seaweed, and salt are placed around the pots. The pit, at Coastal Carolina University, South Carolina, was 5 ft deep, 3 ft wide, and 12 ft long (152 x 91 x 365cm).

3 Reaching the final stage. Wood has to be carefully placed, not dropped onto the pots. Here the last layer of wood is laid on top, with a layer of newspaper and tinder to help get the fire started.

4 The packing can take several hours. When it is complete, the pit is covered with corrugated sheeting before the wood is set on fire.

5 For eight hours the pit is fed with wood and covered, but opened at intervals to allow the fire to travel evenly over the pots throughout the kiln. Here the wood has burned down and the pit is a mass of embers, but the pit is not opened for 36 hours.

6 Two days later. The sides of the pit have collapsed but luckily the pots remain undamaged, the earth being very sandy. At last the pots can be removed, cleaned up, and evaluated.

7 The tactile quality of the pots is enhanced with a coating of beeswax, and the flame marks and colors give each its own personality.

Saggar Firing

A SAGGAR IS A REFRACTORY BOX into which ware is placed for firing. Traditionally a saggar protected pots from flames, gases, and debris, and it was especially necessary when kilns were wood- or coal-fired. Saggars were stacked in tall columns, each stack being known as a "bung."

Modern kilns fire cleanly and saggars are not often used as a matter of necessity, but studio potters have adopted the saggar to create a "microclimate" in the kiln, trapping in smoke and fumes to bring about a local reduction or carbonization, which impacts upon the work inside. Many materials can be included with the fuel in a saggar—salt, metal oxides, and sulfates, for example—to interesting effect.

LOW-TEMPERATURE SAGGAR FIRING

The tall vase being saggar-fired here was previously fired twice—once to biscuit temperature and again with an earthenware crackle glaze inside it. It is placed in a saggar with sawdust, and the saggar goes into a raku kiln (*see page 122*), to be fired outdoors. Any gas-, wood-, or oil-fired kiln is suitable, and the smoke will be carried up the flue. Saggar firing can even be done in an electric kiln, but adequate ventilation is essential, because there will be a good deal of smoke.

(see page 122)

YOU WILL NEED

Biscuit ware
Saggar
Sawdust
Raku kiln

↑ Two examples of low-temperature saggar firing by Gerry Unsworth. The vase on the right was fired at a slightly higher temperature and is more intensely carbonized. There is a visible mark where the sawdust has burned down: a characteristic of saggar firing.

1 This tall form is fired to a low earthenware temperature with an immature glaze inside. This gives rise to a pronounced crackle that will be emphasized by the carbon from the smoke firing.

2 The ware is placed in the saggar with a few handfuls of wood shavings, and the lid is put on. It is fired in a raku kiln, which is heated to 752–1112°F (400–600°C), or until the sawdust catches fire.

3 Through the hole in the top of the kiln, flames can be seen when the sawdust catches fire. The kiln is turned off and left for the sawdust to burn out.

VARIATIONS

Left: *Tall vase biscuit fired, glazed, and fired to earthenware temperature, then sprayed with luster and fired again, this time to 1436°F (780°C). Finally, it was smoked in a saggar firing to 752°F (400°C).* GERRY UNSWORTH

Right: *Vase and bowl in white earthenware clay. The pieces are burnished, and copper luster was applied before firing. A final firing takes place in a saggar in the kiln.* CHRISTINE GITTINS

HIGH-TEMPERATURE SAGGAR FIRING

In this variation, the firing goes to stoneware temperature, 2228°F (1220° C), in a gas kiln. A kiln with a flue is preferable for reasons of ventilation, but this temperature is beyond the reach of most raku kilns. The saggar is made from a clay that is capable of withstanding a degree of thermal shock—crank is a suitable mixture. The saggar needs to be biscuit fired before use. It can be used many times over, but may eventually crack.

The thrown, biscuit-fired porcelain forms shown here are first sprayed thinly with a mixture of manganese dioxide and copper carbonate. Other suitable oxides are iron, copper carbonate, and tin oxide. Apply them thinly and avoid coating the base.

YOU WILL NEED

Biscuit ware
Saggar
Sawdust, fine and coarse
Grain (wheat, rice, etc.)
Gas kiln
Manganese dioxide
Copper carbonate

1 Biscuit-fired porcelain forms were sprayed with a mixture of manganese dioxide and copper carbonate before going into the saggar. This coating is easily scuffed, so a little gum arabic was added to the mix to make it adhere better.

2 Arrange the vessels with care. Pour in the combustible material using a little grain first—underneath the pots rather than in contact with the surface. Fill three-quarters of the saggar and the insides of the pots with fine sawdust or shavings, and top up the fuel level with a thin layer of coarse shavings.

3 Fire the saggar to 2228°F (1220°C) in a gas kiln, with a reduction atmosphere at 1832°F (1000°C). A saggar need not be the only item in the kiln—here, a shelf on top of the saggar acts as a lid and enables another piece to be fired at the same time.

4 The firing is complete. The sawdust burns to ash, leaving a characteristic demarcation line around the pots. There is a change in surface between the bottom of the pots (matte, velvet) and the area above, which will be a glazelike surface with giraffe-skin pattern (*see detail, left*) and, with luck, some areas with rainbow colors!

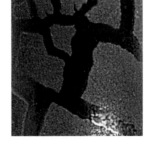

← The finished pieces by Bridget Aldridge. When the forms are cold, remove them from the saggar and wash gently. The excitement of opening a saggar never dwindles—each firing is different, with plenty of scope for experimentation.

THERMAL SHOCK

In some ceramic processes, clay is subjected to sudden changes in temperature as a result of rapid heating or cooling in the firing cycle. Some clays are more able than others to withstand these changes. Crank, a heavily grogged, highly refractory clay, is particularly strong in this respect and also able to cope with multiple firings.

Container Firing with Resist

LIKE MOST KINDS of smoke firing, the method illustrated here is a finishing rather than a firing technique. The temperature reached is insufficient to fire the work, but the action of smoke has a dramatic effect on the surface. Smoking in a container is an easy and safe way to enclose the process and trap the smoke to maximum effect.

A metal garbage can is used, with small holes drilled around its base to produce a slight draft, helping the sawdust to burn.

YOU WILL NEED

Biscuit-fired work to decorate
Masking tape
Garbage can
Sawdust
Newspaper
Furniture wax

1 This slip-cast figure is already biscuit fired. Strips of masking tape are applied to the surface to give soft edges.

2 When all the tape is in place, the figure is placed on a bed of sawdust and newspaper inside the container.

3 More sawdust and newspaper are loosely piled on top of the piece, covering it entirely.

4 The paper at the top of the bin is ignited and allowed to burn. A little lighter fluid can help the combustion process, but never use gasoline or methylated spirits.

5 When the fuel has burned away, the firing is complete. The time taken can vary immensely—this firing took only 15 minutes. To slow the firing, a lid can be placed on the container, or the sawdust can be more densely packed. Slower burning can result in dense black marking instead of the pale smoky effects of rapid combustion.

6 The piece is removed with the aid of gloves, and examined. If the marks are not satisfactory, it can be re-fired—but the masking tape must be reapplied. The piece is cleaned with warm water and a scouring pad.

7 Finally the figure is polished with furniture wax—in this case a tinted "antique pine" wax.

↑ The finished figure by June Taylor, smoke-fired with resist.

A PAPER KILN

This paper kiln, made by Sebastian Blackie, was constructed from very firmly rolled newspapers and is in itself a work of art. It is quite heavy, weighing about 44 lb (20kg), and because of the density of paper it does not burn as rapidly as might be imagined. The insulation properties of the paper are high. During firing the paper forms a fragile carbonized crust, but is not completely consumed. A kiln of similar design has been known to reach 2102°F (1150°C), making this technique a truly alternative firing rather than a method of treating the surface. The decorative effects on pots fired in such a kiln will be various, but will probably be confined to quite subtle smoking marks on the surface.

A paper kiln can be a work of art in its own right! Beside the kiln is the lid, which is tied on after the kiln has been packed.

VARIATIONS

Top right: Bowl burnished, biscuit fired, then patterned with masking tape. The area between the tape was infilled with clay slip. After drying it was placed in a metal container and surrounded with burning newspaper. Beeswax gives a final polish. GEOFF TOWNSEND

Below and below right: Figures and vessel biscuit fired, masked, and container fired, as described opposite. JUNE TAYLOR

HEALTH AND SAFETY

- Sawdust is a highly combustible material. Do not allow it to become airborne, especially near flames—it could provoke an explosion.
- Store sawdust safely.
- Smoke and flying embers are a hazard to people, animals, and property. Check the location of the container, and be aware of the nuisance that smoke and smell can create.
- Avoid firing in windy conditions.
- Always wear a face mask with a fume filter, and heat-resistant gloves.
- Tie back long hair.

SMOKE FIRING

CHAPTER 3

Carbonizing

CLOSELY RELATED to container firing, carbonizing is a means of blackening work by smoke, and can be done with little equipment. Much of the advice on other smoke-firing techniques also applies here—not least of which are the health and safety warnings. Two methods of carbonizing are described here.

YOU WILL NEED

Biscuit ware

Trash can or other fire-resistant container

Hay or sawdust

Slip for resist

1 A container is used for safety reasons, since the fuel is meadow hay and could easily fly away. A lid can be placed over the burning fuel if wished, but there needs to be enough air circulation for it to burn.

2 As a precautionary measure, these biscuit-fired pots were heated in an electric kiln to about 392°F (200°C) so that they were less likely to experience thermal shock. Some slip was splashed onto the surface to act as a resist—it will not adhere to the pots permanently. Pots are placed on a bed of hay, which is lit using a long taper. A barbecue lighter can lend assistance here, if needed.

3 Within 5 or 10 minutes the hay reduces to ash. The pots can be removed as soon as they are cool enough to handle.

4 Buffing with wax polish brings out the color and enriches the surface. Be very careful. On this piece, marks made by grass-seed heads were lost during polishing.

Burnished and carbonized vessel by John Commane, with splashed slip acting as a partial resist to smoke. →

DEEPER BLACK

1 This piece was fired in a raku kiln and taken out with tongs at 1112°F (600°C). It was immediately placed in a container of sawdust and buried with more sawdust, excluding air as much as possible.

2 After 30 minutes or so, the lid is removed and the pot taken out to be quenched in water. (It will still be very hot and can be left in the container longer, if preferred.)

3 The finished piece is washed and buffed with wax polish to a lustrous and slightly metallic sheen. This is the pot made in the Terra Sigillata section, page 72.

← The finished piece by Peter Ilsley. Thrown in red clay with terra sigillata slip applied, then burnished, biscuit fired to 1562°F (850°C), and now carbonized. Wax polish gives a deep sheen.

VARIATIONS

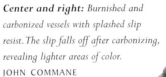

Left: *Small terracotta bowl with burnished rim and incised decoration. It has been lightly smoked to produce contrasting red and blackened areas.*
JO CONNELL

Center and right: *Burnished and carbonized vessels with splashed slip resist. The slip falls off after carbonizing, revealing lighter areas of color.*
JOHN COMMANE

RAKU FIRING

WITH ITS ROOTS IN 16TH-CENTURY JAPAN, the word "raku" freely translates as "enjoyment"—and many potters would agree! The technique of raku has been adapted and developed in the West to cover a variety of firing methods, some of which are illustrated in the following pages. As a general rule, it is a low-temperature earthenware firing, with a rapid firing cycle. Pots are drawn with tongs from the red-hot kiln, and while they are still hot, they can be treated in a number of ways. Often they are plunged into sawdust or other combustible material, or they can be quenched directly in water. Raku firing is appealing for its rapid results, and appears to break all the rules. Because it is such a direct process, bringing the potter so closely in touch with fire and its effects on clay, it has a unique fascination and offers a tremendous learning experience.

BASIC TOOLBOX

Kiln, burner, and gas

Tongs

Reduction containers

Health and safety equipment such as heatproof gloves, face visor, sensible shoes (see page 154)

GLAZED RAKU

Glazed raku is characterized by a pronounced crackle—stained black by carbon if the work is reduced. The crackle is created partly by rapid heating and cooling of the piece, and accentuated by the fact that the glaze—often made from alkaline frit—is likely to be a poor fit to the body. It is susceptible to chipping, and the work almost always remains porous, so it is regarded as nonfunctional.

Raku glazes can be bought or mixed (*see recipes on page 125*). One of the most dramatic colors achievable is a bronze caused by copper in a reduction atmosphere. Silver nitrate is used for yellows/golds, and copper chloride or copper sulfate for turquoise. Many of these chemicals are hazardous, and extreme care is essential in handling them and dealing with the fumes that emit from the kiln.

CLAY BODIES FOR RAKU

The firing process puts a tremendous strain on the clay, and breakages or cracks occur much more frequently than during more conventional firing. Any kind of clay can be used, but it is generally accepted that a more open clay body offers greater resistance to the inevitable thermal shock imposed by the process. Additions of grog, sand, fireclay, or combustible materials (*see page 16*) are likely to increase resilience. Materials

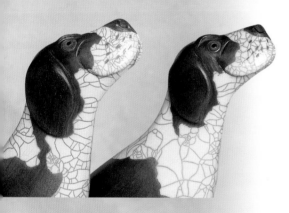

Top: Crank clay vessel with impressed and textured surfaces. Copper raku glaze and raku fired. MERVYN NICHOL

Center: Clay stained with copper carbonate is inlaid into the surface of the bowl, which after biscuit firing, is coated with a white tin glaze. Raku firing has accentuated the crackle of the glaze and shows reduction on the copper-colored clay to red/bronze rather than green. JO CONNELL

Bottom: Raku dogs showing colored glazes including a pronounced white crackle. TONY WHITE

Right: Thrown and altered raku-fired pot. Glazes with base of soft alkaline frit and containing various oxides with copper, brushed and sprayed on. STEPHEN MURFITT

with low expansion and contraction, such as spodumene, petalite, and talc, can lend these properties to clay. Most pottery suppliers carry a raku body, but this will probably be coarse.

KILNS

An electric kiln is not suitable for raku firing, and home building was once the only method. Coal or wood were often used, and kilns were always situated outdoors. Thanks to modern materials, such as ceramic fiber and high thermal insulation brick, it is now possible to buy a purpose-built kiln. Due to its lightness and portability such a kiln may be used under cover, provided there are extraction facilities. Bottled gas is the fuel most often used, because of its convenience.

FIRING

It helps to avoid cracking if pots are warmed prior to firing. Larger pieces can be started off in a cooler kiln and fired more slowly than smaller ones. After the first firing, when the kiln is hot, it can reach temperature again in 30 minutes or so. This, of course, depends on the design of kiln and its efficiency—good insulation and an efficient burner will help.

FORMS SUITABLE FOR RAKU

Forms are less likely to crack if they are:
- Not too thick.
- Of even thickness throughout.
- Without joints.
- Not completely flat—curved forms are stronger.
- Designed so that they can be easily picked up using tongs.

Slip-cast pieces, although often made from a smooth clay, therefore make a good choice, due to their even thickness.

Areas of clay that remain unglazed turn satin black if reduced, or retain the natural color of the biscuit-fired clay if oxidized. The clay color shows to some extent through thin or transparent glaze, and white clay tends to give a brighter base for colors.

Left: Bodypot, dry copper glazed and raku fired using the "covered with container" technique as shown on pages 128–129. CLIVE OATES

HEALTH AND SAFETY

Health and safety are of crucial importance in raku firing. While the process is involving and enjoyable, it is potentially dangerous and must be taken seriously. The author is only too aware of injuries that occurred through carelessness or error, so PLEASE observe the precautions outlined on page 155.

TOP-HAT KILN

Above: This "Top-Hat" kiln was made from an oildrum cleaned of all traces of flammable material. The base is lined with heavy-duty firebrick so that it retains the heat, and the lid with ceramic fiber, which is light and easy to lift. Its design makes the pots easy to remove sideways, making it unnecessary to lean over the hot kiln.

CROSS-DRAFT WOOD-FIRED KILN

1 Flames are drawn from the firebox underneath the chamber and back through the pots, exhausting through the chimney.

2 The door at the side is opened a crack to see whether the glaze has melted on the pots inside. Flames leaping out to grab oxygen indicate a reduction atmosphere in the kiln.

Raku Firing: Reduced

RAKU FIRING IS A TECHNIQUE to which there are many facets and personal interpretations, and potters develop their own methods for success according to desired effects. More often than not, raku-fired pots are subjected to a "post-firing reduction." Reduction is a term frequently encountered in ceramics, and is explained in more detail on page 100. Essentially, reduction is brought about by the incomplete combustion of fuel, caused by the exclusion of air, and produces particular colors and effects in clay and glazes.

Raku-fired pots are reduced by being withdrawn from the kiln when the glaze is fully melted (usually at approximately 1832°F/1000°C), and plunged into combustible material such as sawdust, wood shavings, dry leaves, straw, or shredded paper. There are many variations to the demonstration pictured here. Sometimes work is allowed to cool a little before contacting the sawdust, so that the glaze begins to solidify. This rapid cooling in the open air, or spraying with a little water, can encourage the crackle effect. The reduction can be controlled so that it is heavy (excluding as much oxygen as possible) or light (allowing partial oxidation). One of the biggest problems with raku reduction is the amount of smoke it can generate, so care is needed.

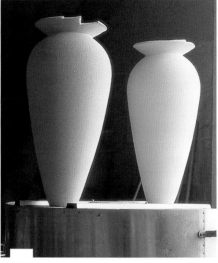

1 The propane gas-fired kiln used here is built in sections, which can be stacked to take work of various shapes and sizes. Pots on top of the kiln are being preheated prior to firing. This reduces some of the thermal shock they experience when placed in the kiln.

2 Now that the glaze has matured, the kiln lid and one top section is removed, and tongs are inserted into the neck of the vessel, ready to lift it out of the kiln.

VARIATIONS

Left: *Raku globe, with white crackle and dry metal glazes. The brass pins were added later.* RICHARD CAPSTICK

Center left: *Clay stained with copper carbonate is inlaid into the surface of this press-molded vessel. A white crackle glaze is applied over the piece, the rim remaining unglazed. Reduction firing has reduced the copper to a rich bronze.* JO CONNELL

Center right: *Flying horse, press-molded and modeled, raku fired with a turquoise crackle glaze, lightly reduced. The unglazed areas are blackened by carbon in the reduction process.* GORDON THOMAS

Far right: *These raku puffins show inventive use of colored glazes and exhibit a characteristic white crackle, made more pronounced by carbon in the reduction process.* TONY WHITE

4 The pot is covered with more sawdust and fired. Flames are visible as the sawdust ignites on contact with the pot.

3 The pot is lowered into the reduction container (an old oildrum) and onto a bed of sawdust.

A finished pot by Stephen Murfitt, showing a strong luster brought out by the reduction process. The glaze used here was high in copper carbonate with a borax frit base. The pot is 17 in (44cm) tall.

5 Because the pot was large it was left for two to three hours in the reduction bin, and is now exposed to cool more. After removal from the container, it will be scrubbed to remove a black carbon deposit and reveal a glowing surface.

RAKU FIRING WITH MIXED MEDIA

Some glazes respond dramatically to reduction—notably those containing copper oxide. Under heavy reduction, this changes from turquoise or green to a reddish bronze. Occasionally though, such colors have been known to reoxidize in the atmosphere over a period of time; the colors revert to greens and lose the luster associated with reduction. The metallic nature of reduced raku glazes is similar to that described in luster reduction (*see page 102*), and the processes for achieving the effects are closely related.

The vase before raku firing. **1** A copper glaze was applied and the piece was fired in a raku kiln to approximately 1832°F (1000°C).

2 The glazed nail vase is taken from the kiln and plunged into sawdust. The glaze contains 3 percent copper carbonate and appears green here until the sawdust has done its work.

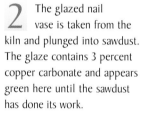

3 Under reduction, the copper turns bronze. The bronze is more pronounced where the pot was in direct contact with the sawdust and therefore became more heavily reduced.

The finished raku-fired, mixed-media vase by Jo Connell.

VARIATION

Right: *Press-molded and slab-built form using staples and nails to join and decorate. Raku fired and reduced with copper glazes added.*
JERRY CAPLAN

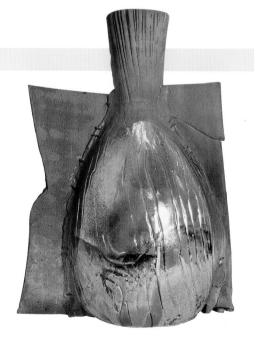

Raku Firing: Oxidized

WHILST MOST RAKU TECHNIQUES involve a degree of reduction, this is not a universal rule. Here we show how raku firing can be oxidized. Put simply, this means that the work is taken out of the kiln and into water or fresh air. It can even be left in the kiln to cool naturally, which can be desirable for delicate or large items. While some of raku's characteristics remain undeveloped by oxidized firing, it is nevertheless an interesting way of using low-temperature glazes, and a crackle in the glaze is inevitable.

CRACKLE

An alkaline-based glaze with additions of copper will produce a rich, crackle turquoise. The same glaze with the addition of 5–10 percent tin oxide will result in a white that will also exhibit a crackle, although it might not be immediately obvious. To bring out the crackle, the pot can be immersed in cold-water fabric dye. Being porous, it will absorb the dye and an intriguing colored crackle will result. India ink is also a good way to bring out the crackle. (*See below for recipes.*)

↑ The copper-glazed pot retains a turquoise green color. If reduced, this glaze would turn bronze and metallic.

3 Two pots are removed from the kiln with tongs when the glaze has melted and are placed on a heatproof surface. They are sprayed with water to assist cooling and to induce a crackle.

1 A low-temperature copper glaze is brushed onto a biscuit-fired pot.

2 A raku kiln, packed with pieces that will be treated in different ways—some can be seen later in this section.

VARIATION

Below: *White tin-glazed bottle with purple crackle caused by immersion in cold-water dye after raku firing.*

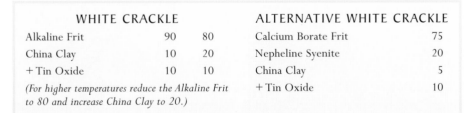

WHITE CRACKLE			ALTERNATIVE WHITE CRACKLE	
Alkaline Frit	90	80	Calcium Borate Frit	75
China Clay	10	20	Nepheline Syenite	20
+ Tin Oxide	10	10	China Clay	5
			+ Tin Oxide	10

(For higher temperatures reduce the Alkaline Frit to 80 and increase China Clay to 20.)

For a clear glaze, omit the tin oxide from either of the above recipes as this makes the glaze opaque. For colored glazes omit all or part of the tin depending on the required opacity, and add:

For deep blue	Cobalt Oxide	1.5%
For turquoise (in oxidation)	Copper Oxide	3%

(*this recipe will produce bronze in reduction conditions*)

Other oxides can be used, and for pastel shades try approximately 5% underglaze color or glaze stain.

Slip Resist With Smoke

THIS METHOD is sometimes known as "naked raku," because it has no glaze, or "smokeless raku," because the smoke can be minimal. Like carbonizing (*see page 118*), it uses the decorative effect produced by smoke. At a temperature around 752–1112°F (400–600°C), work is pulled from the kiln with tongs or heatproof gloves and placed in some kind of reduction chamber. The work can be placed on newspaper or in a container of sawdust—whatever the source of the smoke. Provided it is trapped in, its effect can range from the dramatic to the ethereal.

The resist used for this method is slip, which will not adhere permanently to a biscuit-fired surface, but will stay in place long enough to act as a resist to the smoke. Drawing through the slip leaves channels, which become positive black lines after smoking. Countless variations are possible with this method. Below are some ideas to use as a starting point.

SLIP-RESIST FIRING

In the demonstration below, two pieces are fired, a pot and a bowl, in order to show different decorative approaches. Casting slip is used here, made runny by the addition of a deflocculant (*see page 156*) so that it has a low water content.

YOU WILL NEED

Raku kiln
Biscuit-fired work
Slip / casting slip
Garden wire (optional)
Brushes and sgraffito tools
Metal bin
Sawdust

VARIATIONS TO TRY

- Use different clay bodies, or slip-coated pieces, that will show various colors beneath the resist.
- Remove the pots from the kiln at higher or lower temperatures.
- Smoke the work heavily or lightly, and with different combustible materials.

ALTERNATIVE RESISTS

- Slip made from the same clay as the body.
- Slip with low-melting glaze over the top.
- Slip made from 3 parts china clay to 2 parts flint.
- Pads of biscuit-fired clay stuck to the ware with wet clay or slip.
- Other fire-resistant materials.

1 Casting slip is brushed fairly thickly onto the biscuit-fired bowl, which is held over a pot to catch the excess drips.

2 A few lines are drawn through the slip. The casting slip will quickly begin to shrink and peel off, so it is important to work with speed.

3 A pot is coated thickly with slip in the same way. Smoke will penetrate the slip to produce dark "craze" lines.

4 Plastic-coated garden wire is wrapped around the pot to hold the slip in place as it shrinks and dries.

5 Both pieces are fired to about 1112°F (600°C), removed from the kiln with tongs or strong-quality foundry gloves, and placed on a thin bed of sawdust.

6 More sawdust is sprinkled over them. (A folded sheet of newspaper can be used as an alternative.)

7 A metal lid is placed over to keep in the smoke, and the edges are sealed with sawdust or builders' sand. It is left for at least 20 minutes.

8 The slip falls off the bowl readily to reveal the smoke pattern.

9 On the pot, black lines are evident where the slip shrank and cracked and the smoke penetrated.

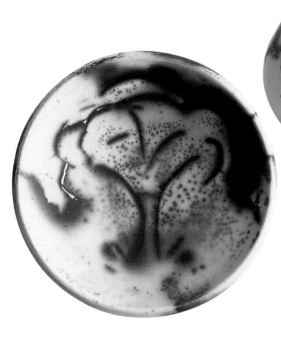

← The smoke effects are subtle and completely individual every time. On the pot, even where no lines were drawn, there is a strong crackle pattern where the slip coating shrank and the smoke made its mark. On the plate, the marks drawn through the slip become dark lines.

ALTERNATIVE METHOD

↑ An alternative method uses a slip coated with low-temperature glaze. The slip prevents the glaze adhering to the body and the entire coating peels away after firing, revealing a crackle of a different nature. This piece has just come out of the firing and has been smoked in a reduction chamber.

127

VARIATIONS

Left: Colored slips on textured clay beneath smoke-fired clay and slip resist.
JOHN COMMANE
Center: Detail of a raku-fired vessel showing sharp contrast as smoke penetrates the shrinking slip coating.
DAVID ROBERTS
Right: Interpretation of a cactus design drawn through slip and fired using the method demonstrated above.
HEATHER MORRIS

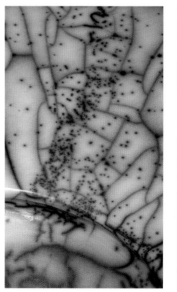

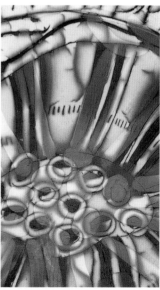

Fumed Raku: Velvet Effects

THE PROCESS OF FUMED RAKU refers to the use of copper oxide and low-temperature firing to create amazing colors on the surface of clay. The copper is usually mixed with flux (see recipe, below) and often contains an agent such as gum arabic, wallpaper paste, or white craft (PVA) glue to protect the surface from scuffing. The mixture is painted or sprayed onto biscuit ware. The ware is removed from the kiln at 1688–1832°F (920–1000°C), and instead of quenching or reducing it, it is placed on a bed of sawdust or other combustible material. This need only be a tiny amount, just enough to ignite when hot pots are placed on top of it. Paint remover sprinkled onto the sawdust beforehand can aid ignition, so that a few flames lick around the pots and cause interesting patterns. The heat is sealed in with a lid, and fuming occurs inside the chamber.

Fuming is another technique that potters can adapt to their individual needs, and even the tiniest nuances in the method can make an enormous difference to the result.

1 Here, the fuming mixture is painted on, but it could be applied by any of the usual methods. Spraying is a favorite, since it gives an even and controllable coating—but the mixture is heavy so it can block the spray gun.

5 Here, a light spraying with a hose cools the metal lid so that it can be opened sooner. An optional step for impatient potters!

FUMING VARIATIONS

• Vary the temperature at which work is removed from the kiln: lower temperatures tend to give purple and pinks, higher temperatures give more metallic effects, including gold/yellow.

• Latex resist (*see page 126*) underneath the fuming mixture can create contrast between the dark yellowish-green "petroleum" colors and a matte gray/black body.

• After firing, a small jewelry torch can be directed onto the surface to create localized circular patterns, because the copper will remain sensitive to heat. Unfortunately, it is all too easy to crack the work in this way—so be cautious! Effects can also be incised or scratched.

• Allow a short burst of oxygen into the chamber at different stages in the fuming process, exercising the greatest care at all times (*see page 154*).

FUMING MIXTURE

Copper Oxide	90
Alkaline Frit	10
+ Bentonite	10
+ Wallpaper Paste	1

VARIATIONS

Left: *Form made from crank clay that was press-molded. The surfaces are impressed and textured.*
MERVYN NICHOL

Center left: *A fuming mixture, similar to the recipe above, was applied to this piece and after raku firing, it was withdrawn from the kiln and buried in sawdust.* CLIVE OATES

Center right: *Seahorse, slipcast in white earthenware, biscuit fired and fumed.* CLAIRE BOTTERILL

Right: *Thrown vessel, fumed with copper oxide as above.* HARRY DANCEY

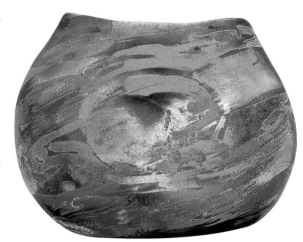

2 At a temperature of 1688–1832°F (920–1000°C), the pot is removed from the kiln and placed on a bed of sawdust, which ignites immediately. (Pyrometers are rarely accurate in these circumstances, so you need to become familiar with your kiln and experiment with different temperatures.)

3 A lid is placed over the container immediately, and is then left for a few minutes.

4 The lid is then lifted just enough to allow in a burst of air, and quickly dropped back into place. It is sealed with sawdust (or builders' sand) and left to cool.

6 The lid is now removed. At this stage the pots cool rapidly in the open air since, unlike raku reduction, there is not enough sawdust to act as insulation.

7 The pot is cooled in water, washing off any sawdust residue. Quenching in water is optional.

↑ The finished piece by Tony Blenkinsopp. Many decorative effects are achievable using the method described. The pots will remain porous however, and are therefore not suitable for food use.

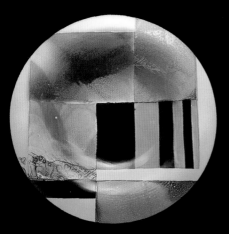
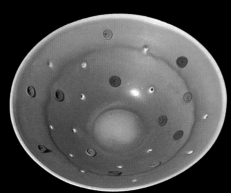
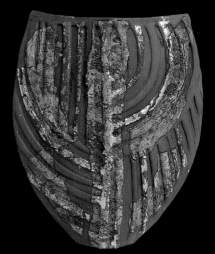

Chapter 4 MULTIPLE FIRINGS AND POST-FIRING TECHNIQUES

Most ceramic processes require one or two firings, but sometimes it is necessary to fire a piece several times. On-glaze enamels and precious metal lusters need at least a third firing—and occasionally many more. The following pages also offer ideas for treating "finished" ceramics to additional layers of decoration and firing, and the destruction of surfaces by gritblasting.

ON-GLAZE ENAMELS AND OTHER PIGMENTS

Glazed and fired ceramics are usually regarded as "finished," but this need not be the case. Additional pigments can be applied, demanding a third firing. In this section, we look at ways of applying enamels (known as on-glaze color or on-glaze enamel) on fired ceramic surfaces.

Enamels are low-fired glazes that are usually applied to a glazed surface and then fired to 1292–1562°F (700–850°C). A glazed surface is not, however, essential as a base for enamels and studio potters often use these colors on unconventional backgrounds (*see* Painting Enamels, *page 134*).

see Painting Enamels, *page 134*

BASIC TOOLBOX

Enamel colors: in powder or ready-mixed form

Suitable medium, brushes, etc.

Decal paper, covercoat solution, and screen print materials and equipment

Ready-glazed pots: white ware

FIRING ENAMELS

Because enamels are made from a variety of pigments, not all colors fire at the same temperature. Some are fugitive at higher temperatures, especially reds and oranges, often based on cadmium and selenium. Several firings may be needed for a multicolored piece, starting with the highest firing color. Enamels are widely used in the ceramics industry, some hand-painted pieces (notably Royal Crown Derby, which also incorporates gold into the design) being fired a dozen times or more.

The optimum temperature depends to an extent on the base glaze to which the enamels are applied, so check suppliers' recommendations. The glaze softens and combines with the enamel to form a permanent finish, though the surface is not as hard as most glazes, and continued abrasion or dishwashing may eventually damage the surface.

Left: "Jelly-go-round." Two-piece jelly mold with on-glaze enamels and transfer prints on slip-cast earthenware. LAURA VICKERS

Top: "Signpost." Slip-cast earthenware piece with underglaze decoration. Sheets of flat on-glaze color were cut up and applied as decals on top of the glaze, and given a third firing. ANDREW DOCHERTY
Center: Bowl with on-glaze enamels painted onto a background of colored slips previously fired to 2282°F (1250°C) but without glaze. STEPHANIE REDFERN
Bottom: "Tutti Frutti." Slab-built, impressed with a wooden fruit block, and stained with high-temperature red stain. The transfers were gold luster, and the piece was fired several times. PHILOMENA PRETSELL

APPLICATION OF ENAMELS

Enamels can be applied in a number of ways, as demonstrated in the following pages:

- Painting (using a variety of mediums).
- Printing. Screen printing is the most common way, but stamping and sponging can also be used (*see page 137*).
- As decals (*see page 138*).
- Ground laying—the dusting of powdered enamel onto a sticky, oiled surface.
- Spraying. With care, runs can be avoided on a glossy surface by warming up the object so that moisture quickly evaporates. The addition of a little PVA glue to the enamel mixture may also be helpful for adhesion.

The following chart may serve as a guide for firing temperatures.

Type of Ware	Temp °F	Temp°C
Earthenware	1292–1472	700–800
Stoneware or porcelain	1436–1544	780–840

USE OF ENAMELS

The colors used in the manufacture of enamels are derived from the usual metal oxides employed in ceramics. Like other glazes, enamels are based on alumina, silica, and a flux. A wide range of bright colors are available, that are not traditionally within the studio potter's palette. Some colors are intermixable and may be lightened or darkened by additions of white or black enamel—but check with the supplier, or experiment. In some cases it may be possible to fire luster and enamels simultaneously.

Above: *Tall stoneware vase (2 ft / 60cm high) decorated with decals and given a third firing.* WILL LEVI MARSHALL

STUDIO OR INDUSTRIAL

Enamels are often associated with industrial ceramics, but the barriers are coming down, and studio potters often combine the industrial approach with studio techniques to make exciting work. It can be instructive to take a tour around the decorating department of a large ceramics factory to observe the on-glaze methods that are widely used in the industrial domain. One of the challenges of using enamels is to make this final surface application appear an integral part of the process rather than an afterthought. With practice and sensitive use of the materials, this can be achieved.

Enamels are also found in allied crafts, such as glass and metalwork. Though their composition varies, they are similarly low-firing, glass-like materials, which can be brightly colored, vibrant, and glossy.

Left: Decorative teapot, earthenware glazed, with added decals bought directly from industrial suppliers, and mixed media details. VIRGINIA GRAHAM

ENAMEL VARIATIONS

- Mix enamel with underglaze color to make it less glossy.
- Fire enamel to a higher temperature, so that it sinks into the glaze. While some colors may be lost if over-fired, others will give a pleasingly soft and blended effect.
- Use varied combinations of enamel or oxide on a glazed surface and re-fire to approximately the temperature of the original glaze. This will form an "in-glaze" decoration (*see page 136*).

Painting Enamels

IN THIS EXAMPLE, enamels add defining touches to a design that is almost complete. The fish was already partially decorated and fired to stoneware temperature. Before firing, fine lines were incised into the clay surface as decorative details, delineating areas to be painted later with enamels. When the work was dry, a copper carbonate and water mixture was painted on and dusted off again (this method is described in more detail on page 96).

Although enamels are normally referred to as "on-glaze," this example uses only a little glaze, painted onto small areas, just to add sparkle to the fish. The aim was to give a softer effect than that usually associated with enamel colors. Painted fairly thinly onto a matte background, the enamels are subtle, and in some areas they represent more of a wash than a dense, flat covering. The result is far removed from the brash colors often associated with industrially applied enamel. Enamels must be applied to clean, non-greasy surfaces, in a dustfree environment.

YOU WILL NEED

Work to decorate

On-glaze enamel colors, ready mixed, or powder with suitable mediums

Brushes

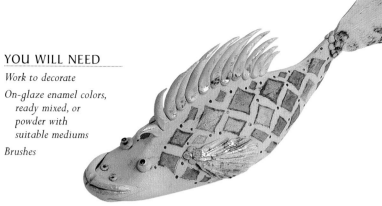

↑ Fish, by Stephanie Redfern. Fired to stoneware temperature, painted with enamel colors, and fired again to 1382°F (750°C).

1 This piece was press-molded with modeled additions. Before painting with enamels the fish was fired to stoneware temperature (2282°F/1250°C), with only touches of glaze applied to highlight the detailed areas.

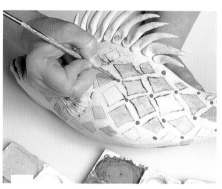

2 The enamel powders are mixed with a water-based medium and thinned with water as necessary. Applied thinly, the color will fire with only a gentle sheen. If painted on thickly it may appear more shiny. Light pencil marks may be used as a guide.

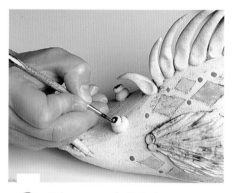

3 Colors are gradually built up to enhance the decorative qualities of the fish. The enamel colors form an interesting contrast with the matte clay body and introduce an extra decorative dimension.

VARIATIONS

Right: All these pieces are hand built, decorated with colored slips and oxides, and fired to 2282°F (1250°C) before being decorated with on-glaze enamel colors and re-fired to 1382°F (750°C).
STEPHANIE REDFERN

Decorating White Ware

WHITE WARE IS THE NAME given in the industry to white pottery and tiles that are left undecorated. Often these items can be bought as substandard pieces that did not reach the decorating stage. They can be earthenware, porcelain, or bone china. They are mostly suitable for re-firing to a lower temperature for enamel or luster decoration, with oxides or with applications of another glaze (especially a brush-on glaze). Following are three of the many methods of applying decoration to finished white ware.

OXIDE COATING

These white bathroom tiles were coated with red iron oxide and scratched through to give the impression of a woodcut.

YOU WILL NEED
Glazed tiles
Oxides or brush-on glazes
Brushes
Sgraffito tools
Wallpaper paste (optional)

1 Red iron oxide is mixed with water and painted on with a broad brush. Adding a little wallpaper paste to the mixture can assist adhesion. The oxide could also be mixed with a small quantity of earthenware glaze to help it flow in the firing. Other oxides can be used. It is simply a matter of experimentation and color choice.

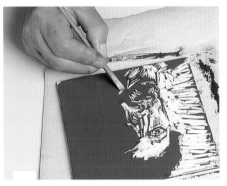

2 After drying (a hairdryer can speed the process), any suitable tool can be used to cut through the coating. Here a chisel-pointed wooden modeling tool is used.

3 The process of removing oxide from the surface creates an effect similar to wood or linocut, part of the background being deliberately left behind to emphasize the tool marks.

4 A piece of paper catches excess oxide, which can be reused. Care must be taken not to touch the surface until it is fired, as it is very fragile.

↑ The finished piece, by Malcolm Unsworth, was fired to 1976°F (1080°C), at which temperature the glaze on the tile begins to melt and the iron oxide sinks well into the surface.

SURFACE APPLICATIONS FOR WHITE WARE

- On-glaze enamels
- Lusters
- Oxides
- Glazes (especially brush-on glazes)

VARIATION

Below: *Brush-on glazes can be used to decorate green ware (unfired), biscuit ware, and also glazed ceramics. This glazed tile was first trailed with hot wax lines using a Tjanting tool (see Painting Glazes, page 92) and then the areas between the wax were filled in with colored glaze. It was fired to 1976°F (1080°C).*

PAINTING ENAMELS ON WHITE WARE

Enamels can be applied in many ways to the surface of a mature glaze and then re-fired to an appropriate temperature. The optimum temperature for this firing depends to an extent on the glaze beneath—higher-fired white ware such as porcelain will require a higher enamel firing. An average enamel firing will be around 1382°F (750°C). Two methods of application are illustrated here.

BANDING

↑ This method of painting (also seen on page 64) is an excellent way to apply color to the rim of a plate. A layer of cork is attached to the banding wheel so that the plate will not slip as it is rotated. The fingers "walk" around the stem of the wheel while the loaded brush is held against the plate. This time a water-based medium is used.

↑ A decal is applied (see page 138) with care not to damage the banded rim, and the plate is fired to 1382°F (750°C). A water-based medium is more vulnerable to damage, so it can be fired on for permanency before decals are added, and then fired once more. Banded and decaled plate by Ken Whittingham.

YOU WILL NEED
For banding
Banding wheel
White ware to decorate
Water-based paint
Decal
Paintbrush
For painting
White ware to decorate
Ready-mixed enamels or enamel powder and oil-based medium
Paintbrush

TIP

Some white ware will fire more successfully than others—try to use new clean pots where possible. Ware which is old has often absorbed dirt, and moisture will have to escape during firing. This can result in black carbon spots under the glaze. It can be cured to an extent by drilling tiny holes in the glaze (underneath, where they cannot be seen) to allow impurities to escape.

This bone china cup and saucer is now ready for firing to 1382°F (750°C). The colors will then appear glossy. →

PAINTING

↑ China painting is a subject in its own right, and this is just a glimpse of its possibilities. Painting on the shiny glazed surface is a skill that needs practice. Ready-mixed enamels can be used for painting, or enamel powder can be mixed with a suitable medium. Here, an oil-based medium of turpentine and fat oil is used. The powder is first mixed with turpentine and then thickened with fat oil to the right consistency.

VARIATIONS

Below: This image was drawn onto a plate with a mapping pen using powdered black enamel mixed with glycerin. The ink does not dry until it is fired on.
Right: A commercially made, glazed wall tile painted with enamels using a water-based medium and re-fired to 1382°F (750°C).

DIRECT SCREEN PRINTING

The next section on decals (*page 138*) deals with the making of a screen using the photo silk screen technique. Here, a screen produced in the same way is used to print directly onto glazed tiles, without the need for the interim process of transfers.

(*page 138*)

YOU WILL NEED

Screen
Gummed paper tape
Squeegee
Enamel and water-based medium
Palette knife

1 On-glaze enamel is mixed with a water-based medium. (Oil-based medium is usually used for decals but new water-based systems are coming onto the market, and are preferable for reasons of health and safety.)

2 The image on the screen is taped with the gummed paper tape used to stretch watercolor paper. It defines the parameters of an image which is not square on the screen and which is too large for the tile. The tape reduces the area to be printed and helps to square up the print.

3 Sticks are used to raise the screen above the tile so that the screen can spring back once the ink is squeegeed. The tile sits in a square window cut out of cardboard. This helps with positioning and creates a level, step-free surface on which to print. The tile is re-fired to 1382°F (750°C).

↑ Willow-pattern patio table by Jo Connell, 24 in (61cm) in diameter and 3 ft (91cm) high. The tiles were cut and rearranged as a mosaic.

137

VARIATIONS

Left: *This set of honey-glazed floor tiles is adapted from a design from the 15th or 16th century. They were screen printed with iron oxide mixed with a water-based medium, using a coarse mesh screen. The tiles were re-fired to 1976°F (1080°C) so that the glaze itself melted and the iron oxide sank into the glaze.*
Top right: *A skeleton poplar leaf was placed under a screen coated with photo-sensitive emulsion and exposed on a light bed. The resulting screen was used to print this green-glazed tile several times with the delicate leaf design, using dark blue enamel, fired to 1382°F (750°C).*
Bottom right: *This design was screen printed in dark blue / green enamel on a commercially made, vitrified quarry tile, and re-fired to 1382°F (750°C).*

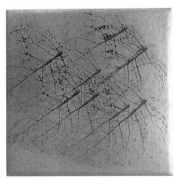

ON-GLAZE ENAMELS AND OTHER PIGMENTS

CHAPTER 4

Decals

DECALS OR TRANSFERS can be made using enamels in conjunction with the silk screen-printing process (*see page 52*). Making decals is exacting and time-consuming, and demands certain facilities, but it is not really difficult. There are companies that will make up decals for you if the artwork is supplied, or decals can be bought in ready-made sheets. It is possible to make multicolored decals, and the main consideration then is the exact registration of one color with another. A fresh screen needs to be used for each color, and each must be carefully aligned with the next. For the purposes of our demonstration, the decals have been made in one color only.

YOU WILL NEED

Silk screen
Light exposure bed
Light-sensitive emulsion
Coating trough
Squeegee
Decal paper
On-glaze enamel and suitable medium
Covercoat and brush
Glazed ware to decorate
Rubber kidney palette

MAKING DECALS

1 First an image is generated. Here, we made black-and-white photocopies of illustrations of fishes. By cutting and pasting, a master copy is arrived at. This is scanned on the computer, or photocopied, and printed onto acetate (the "film"). A film can be made in other ways—a drawing can be done directly onto transparent film, for example. An alternative method is to brush paint remover onto the back of thin photocopy paper, rendering it transparent enough for the photo silk screen process which is used here.

2 A screen is coated with light-sensitive emulsion. A trough is used to spread the emulsion evenly across the mesh. For printing enamels, a fine mesh should be used (80-120T). The screen is placed in a dark drying cabinet for about 10 minutes before being exposed on a light bed.

3 A light bed uses mercury vapor lamps to expose the emulsion, in conjunction with a vacuum to bring the screen and the film in close contact with each other.

After exposure the screen is washed. A negative image will have been left behind on the screen. **4**

5 The emulsion will act as a resist, allowing ink through where the image remains unblocked by the emulsion. The image is printed with ceramic ink, using a squeegee.

6 The ink is on-glaze enamel mixed with an oil-based medium. Water-based media are becoming available and are more convenient to use than oil-based types. The paper has a special gummed surface for decals. Printing is best done on a vacuum bed, which has a suction device to hold the paper still.

7 When the print is dry (an hour at least), it can be painted over with a film of "covercoat," a plastic-like coating (in this case, yellow) that adheres to the surface. This must also be allowed to dry. Decals should be stacked only when absolutely dry, with sheets of waxed paper between them.

APPLYING DECALS

Decals can be applied easily to smooth, glazed surfaces using the method described below. They are then fired to a temperature appropriate to both the decal and the glaze beneath—approximately 1382°F (750°C). It is important to work in a dust-free environment so that no grit or dirt becomes trapped underneath the decal.

YOU WILL NEED

Homemade or bought decals

Glazed item for decorating

Rubber kidney palette

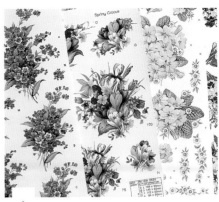

Commercially prepared decals are available from ceramic color suppliers. If you wish to produce colorful and intricate designs, it is often simpler to buy decals rather than make them yourself.

1 The paper transfer is trimmed close to the image with scissors and floated in clean, warm water for a few minutes until the gummed paper softens and slides easily off the back.

2 The decal, now just the top plastic film with image attached, is slid onto the glazed surface. Using a rubber kidney palette and smoothing from the center of the image, all air and moisture is expelled and the image is firmly attached. It is now ready to fire, and the yellow covercoat will burn away completely.

VARIATIONS

Below: Stoneware dishes fired at 2336°F (1280°C) then decorated with multi-patterned decals and fired once again, this time at the lower temperature of 1382°F (750°C). WILL LEVI MARSHALL

← Two fish decals on a plate banded with on-glaze enamel, fired to 1382°F (750°C).

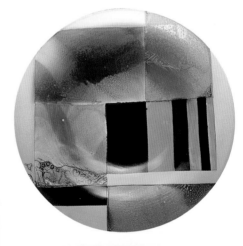

APPLYING DECALS TO A CURVED SURFACE

1 A decal applied to a curved surface needs a little more care. Covercoat has a certain amount of flexibility, but when the curve becomes compound (curves in more than one direction), decals tend to wrinkle.

2 As with a flat surface, a rubber kidney palette is used to carefully expel all moisture and any air bubbles from beneath the decal. Once the decal is firmly attached, the piece is ready to fire.

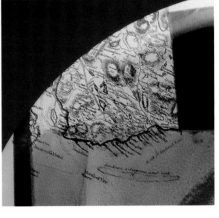

LUSTERS: OXIDIZED

LUSTER CAN BE ACHIEVED BY USING a combination of key materials together with tight control of the kiln atmosphere, which must at some point be reducing (*see* Luster Reduction Firing, *page 102*). The effect is magical though elusive—but there is an easier way! Commercially prepared lusters can be applied to the surface of a fired, finished glaze, and be fired again to a low temperature in an oxidizing kiln. Lusters are a means of developing a wide range of decorative colors and metallic effects on mature glazed surfaces. They are reliable and easy to apply, and the majority of contemporary lusterware is produced this way.

These commercial lusters are chemically complex. They carry their own reducing agent which burns off in an oxidizing firing and achieves local reduction. Because the reducing agent used is a natural resin, they are also known as "resin lusters"—they have a distinctive aroma, due to the use of various pungent resins such as camphor. All these resonates have a similar brown "treacle" appearance so it is difficult to distinguish between them in their unfired form. During firing, the resin burns away and as the temperature rises the glaze beneath begins to soften. At this stage, a very thin film of metal or metal oxide is deposited on the surface and a bond is formed between metal and glaze. It is important to fire high enough for this bond to develop, otherwise the luster may not adhere adequately to the surface and will be easily worn away if subject to abrasion.

FIRING TEMPERATURES

Like on-glaze enamel, luster fires just below the softening point of the glaze to which it is applied, thus ensuring adhesion to the glaze. Depending on the maturing temperature of the base glaze, it will require a temperature as low as 1112°F (600°C) for low-fired glazes, and as high as 1742°F (950°C) for stoneware or porcelain, but there are many variable factors and optimum temperatures are best discovered through experiment. The chart of firing temperatures on page 141 can be taken as a guide.

BASIC TOOLBOX

Lusters

Luster thinners (sometimes known as essence)

Brushes

Spray equipment

Top: Porcelain bottle with matte green glaze, reduction fired. Delicately painted and banded with a fine brush using liquid bright-gold and purple luster. MARY RICH

Center: Bowl with sprayed luster over a crackle earthenware glaze. Luster firing 1256°F (680°C). GERRY UNSWORTH

Bottom: Black glazed, commercially produced tile, sponge stamped with mixed lusters and re-fired to 1436°F (780°C).

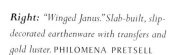

Right: "Winged Janus." Slab-built, slip-decorated earthenware with transfers and gold luster. PHILOMENA PRETSELL

LUSTER FIRING TEMPERATURES

Type of glazed ware	Firing Range °F	Firing Range °C
Glass	840–1015	450–550
Majolica type glazes	1110–1295	600–700
Tiles & low fired earthenware	1110–1560	600–850
Standard earthenware	1295–1560	700–850
China	1295–1650	700–900
Porcelain	1295–1690	700–950

(Courtesy of Charles Lamb)

A glazed surface is not an absolute requirement, and exciting effects can be obtained by applying luster to an unglazed surface (*see* Painted and Sprayed Luster, *pages 142–143*). The unglazed surface may also be porous and perhaps burnished and/or smoked. Applied in this way the effects will be more soft and subtle, with less sharply defined areas of color.

PREPARED LUSTERS AND PRECIOUS METALS.

The resins and oils in commercial lusters modify their brushing and leveling properties, as well as the viscosity and drying time. They can also be fired onto glass, and historically they were first used in this way. An astonishing range of colors is available, giving a wide range of decorative metallic and iridescent effects on mature glazed surfaces.

Iridescent lusters produce a "pearlized" finish, like soap bubbles or mother of pearl. Precious metals are also often given the general term "lusters" and can be applied in the same ways described here. These are opaque and come in gold (burnishing gold, bright gold, gold luster, etc), platinum, bronze, and copper forms. They are generally more expensive than iridescent lusters, though inexpensive metallic forms are available.

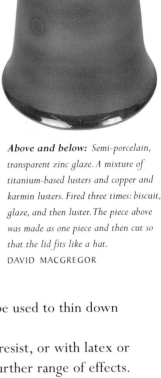

Above and below: *Semi-porcelain, transparent zinc glaze. A mixture of titanium-based lusters and copper and karmin lusters. Fired three times: biscuit, glaze, and then luster. The piece above was made as one piece and then cut so that the lid fits like a hat.*
DAVID MACGREGOR

APPLICATION

Lusters can be applied in many ways, some of which are outlined in the following pages. Brushing, spraying (air brushing), or stamping/sponging are commonly used. Luster can also be screen printed, either directly or via the "decal" process. It is

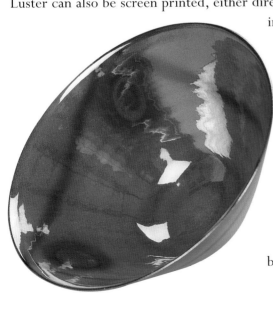

important to use the correct type of luster medium and thinners recommended by suppliers. These can be used to thin down lusters, which may thicken on standing.

Used with a commercially prepared resist, or with latex or gouache as resist, luster can achieve a further range of effects. Crackle effects too can be created by painting a prepared mixture over areas of unfired luster. Petrol, paraffin, thinners, or detergent can be dabbed or sprayed on to break up the unfired surface in an interesting way.

Luster should be applied in a dust-free environment and allowed to dry for an hour or so before firing. Luster decoration may be damaged by abrasion and dishwashing as the surface coating is so thin.

Painted and Sprayed Luster

LUSTER CAN BE APPLIED in different ways according to the desired effect. Brushwork can be used to produce fine detail and a variety of individualized luster effects. When using brushwork the surface must be very smooth—in the example shown on the right, the luster is applied to a finely prepared, unglazed porcelain, hand-built form.

An overall luster can be obtained by spraying. A small, high-quality spray gun or an airbrush is used, and the piece to be sprayed must be clean and dry. Grease and dust can interfere with the process, so cleanliness is essential throughout. Cotton gloves can help to avoid fingermarks beforehand, and the work must not be handled at all after spraying—it can be placed on a tile for support. It is important to use the medium and thinners recommended by the manufacturer, but an accidental mixture can sometimes give pleasing results. Spraying can be combined with brushwork and other methods.

In the example of sprayed luster demonstrated below, the bowl was glazed with a crackle glaze before spraying. As the luster tries to level out, it "sags" into the crackle, accentuating the effect.

YOU WILL NEED

Pre-fired work to decorate

Range of commercially prepared lusters

Brushes and / or spray facilities

Luster resist or gouache paint

PAINTED LUSTER

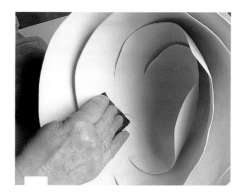

1 The bowl is fired to 2246°F (1230°C) without glaze, and rubbed down with fine (grade 60) carborundum paper, using the wet-and-dry method.

SPRAYED LUSTER

↑ A crackle-glazed earthenware bowl is sprayed with luster.

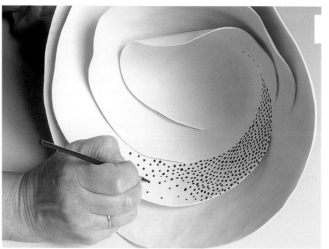

2 A proprietary luster resist is applied as dots and then left to dry. Designer's gouache can be used as a substitute. These dots will appear white when the piece is fired.

↑ Fired and finished blue lustered bowl by Gerry Unsworth: fired to 1976°F (1080°C) with earthenware glaze, sprayed with luster, and fired again to 1256°F (680°C).

VARIATIONS

Left: *Porcelain bowl with inlay, glaze, lusters, and gold.* LES RUCINSKI
Center left: *Porcelain bottle, painted with liquid bright gold using a very fine brush. An example of the detail achievable by careful application.* MARY RICH
Center right: *Low-fired sprayed luster bowl with crackle glaze.* GERRY UNSWORTH
Right: *Terra cotta bowl, partially glazed and with gold luster added, using a medium to produce a crackle effect.* LES RUCINSKI

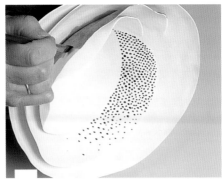

3 Larger areas of luster are applied directly using a soft but springy brush. Lusters in jars appear nothing like their fired colors so it is important to keep a record of what colors you are using.

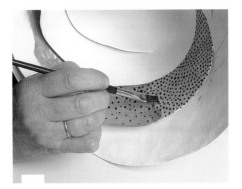

4 Luster is painted over the dried resist. As luster is expensive it is wise to keep a brush for each color—this avoids wasting time and luster by cleaning brushes in between applications.

5 More luster is applied to the ground color with a fine brush, dipped first in luster and then in gasoline. This disperses the luster and gives a "bleeding" effect.

6 With a complicated shape such as this piece, it is advisable to allow the luster to dry before moving on to another section.

Bowl by Maria Stewart, with completed decoration. The color has changed totally in firing. Without a glaze the luster has definite and delicate metallic appearance. Fired to 1337°F (725°C).

Stamped and Sponged Luster

STAMPING IS AN INTRIGUING WAY of applying luster to a glazed or unglazed surface. The example uses a pencil eraser and a dense type of sponge similar to the synthetic rubber used in diving suits. These are cut to shape and mounted on a wooden "stalk" for easy handling.

Colors can be blended or overlapped by stamping, and other methods of application can be combined with it. Resist methods can make use of luster resist (*see* Painted Luster, *pages 142-143*), latex (masking fluid), or designer's gouache, which can be scrubbed off after firing. Luster is applied to earthenware glaze in this example, but the background can be a glaze of any temperature—or no glaze at all.

YOU WILL NEED

Pre-fired work to decorate—tiles or handmade work, glazed or not
Selection of lusters
Sponge or pencil eraser to cut for stamps
Excise knife or craft knife

↑ Shown above are a selection of lusters, sponges, and stamps. Dispense small amounts of luster as they are expensive and only a little is needed for this method.

STAMPED LUSTER

1 Lusters are first poured onto a tile, which acts as a palette. Since they look similar, they will need to be labeled for identification.

2 A sponge is dipped into the luster until thinly coated, then stamped on a white glazed commercial tile. To avoid skin contact with the luster, surgical gloves are worn.

3 A pencil eraser is used to make a different kind of mark. The denseness of the rubber means that the luster is applied more thickly than with a sponge.

↑ Tiles with stamped leaves, fired to 1436°F (780°C) in an electric kiln.

VARIATIONS

Left: *Slip coated, burnished, and lustered using stamps and resist techniques. This piece was finally smoked by raku firing giving subtle and ethereal effects.* ANNE JAMES

Center: *Platinum, copper, and mother-of-pearl luster has been applied to a gloss black glazed tile and a matte blue glazed tile, demonstrating the effects of luster on both matte and gloss surfaces.*

Right and far right: *Black stoneware forms with delicate on-glaze luster decoration applied by stamping.* JOHN WHEELDON

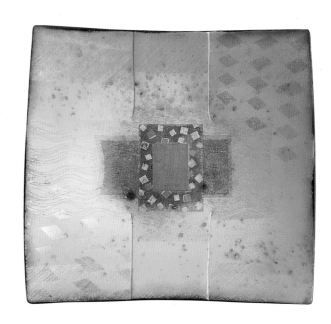

SPONGED LUSTER

A dense sponge is preferable for small, accurate stamps. Masking tape is stuck to the surface to make it more rigid, and a geometry instrument is used against which to brace the excise knife so that it cuts accurately into the sponge. The masking tape is then removed.

1 Copper, platinum, and mother-of-pearl lusters are stamped onto a satin green, stoneware glazed dish.

↑ A finished piece by John Commane. The bowl was originally fired to 2282°F (1250°C) after coating with manganese dioxide. After lusters were applied it was re-fired to 1436°F (780°C).

The outside is stamped too. **2**

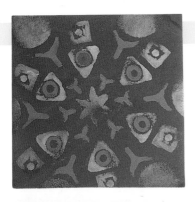

POST-FIRING TECHNIQUES

THE HARD AND DURABLE NATURE of fired ceramics lends itself to a wide variety of post-firing treatments, ranging from gilding with metal leaf to texturing by aggressive means, such as gritblasting (also known as sandblasting). These techniques are more appropriate for nonfunctional items, from small-scale jewelry to larger sculptural pieces. There are no bounds to the inventiveness of the maker who is willing to explore an idea to the extreme of possibly destroying the ceramics in a quest for a surface quality or effect!

BASIC TOOLBOX

Gritblaster and resists: tape, latex, white (PVA) glue

Metal leaf, gold size

The mixed media gallery brings us full circle to the idea that ceramic surfaces can be closely allied to so many other materials. The versatile nature of clay lends itself to assemblage with metal, wood, glass, fabric, rubber, and found objects—there is no limit to the variations achievable.

Mixing ceramics with other materials is not a new idea. During the later part of the sixteenth century the additions of silver mounts and lids on salt-glaze jugs and mugs was adopted by English traders to give added value to the imported wares. Later, a few German potters designed some of their products especially for the addition of pewter lids and mounts.

Steve Harrison's work (*see page 152*) echoes this tradition and he applies details in silver and hard woods to his salt-glaze pieces. His creamware pieces also have the addition of silver parts along with salt-glazed knobs and handles, thereby mixing two types of ceramic, from very different firings, in a highly individual way. There are many other examples of materials used in a complementary way with clay, some to be seen on pages 152–153. Other successful combinations frequently made by studio potters include turned wooden lids for jars, or platters for cheese covers; ceramic handles for cutlery; ceramic tiles set into wooden furniture, or ceramic knobs for doors and drawers.

The following list of "non-ceramic treatments" offers some ideas for those wishing to use ceramics in a less traditional and often nonfunctional

Top: *Sail form in bone china on a stoneware base. The piece was sandblasted using a latex mask. The artist makes use of the hard, crisp edge created by eroding bone china in conjunction with a resist.*
PETER BEARD

Center: *Formed in a mold, this piece was smoked inside an incinerator with newspaper after biscuit firing. Gold leaf was applied after firing.*
JOY BOSWORTH

Bottom and right: *"Hidden Cheetah" bowl and animal jars in blasted porcelain. This artist uses blasting in a very precise and linear way, which belies the hard, unyielding nature of the fired clay she decorates.* DIMITRA GRIVELLIS

Above: Gritblasting cabinets are available in many sizes and you should purchase one to suit the work you will be doing. An appropriate compressor will be needed to drive the blast gun. A grit size of 40 (for coarse blasting) to 100 (for finer surface effects) is recommended.

manner. While the notion of such treatment may be anathema to many potters, in the realm of ceramic sculpture and fine art ceramics can be used in very unconventional ways!

- Clear or stained waxes (furniture wax, beeswax, boot polish) seal a porous surface and enhance the sheen on burnished ware (*see page 35*, Burnishing).
- Acrylic varnish (available as a spray) can seal the surface of porous ceramics, enabling a piece to hold water (useful on smoked ware).
- Indian ink rubbed into a crackle glaze is an excellent way to accentuate the effect, which indeed may not even be visible without it.
- Fabric dyes produce a similar effect and provide a wider color range. They are particularly effective on porous crackle-glazed or unglazed ware.
- Etching paste (available from glass suppliers) can remove the gloss from a glaze and is useful in conjunction with a resist—it can even be screen printed. Use with care and according to the instructions.
- Metallic "gilding" creams and waxes are used for restoration of picture frames, furniture, and architectural details. These can add an effective touch of gold, silver, pewter, or brass to highlight specific areas, especially on sculptural pieces.
- Resins—castable resins make interesting additions to clay, being translucent and of glass/glaze-like appearance. Resins are often used in the restoration of ceramics, as they can be colored and textured to match the original ceramic.
- Textured paint, such as Artex applied over biscuit ware, forms an interesting surface capable of withstanding smoke-firing temperatures. An accidental discovery!
- Fired porcelain can form an interesting background for watercolor painting, providing a durable, bright, white surface. Sgraffito lines may be inscribed before firing and painting.
- A copper verdigris effect is seen on page 150 used by Peter Hayes as a "weathering" effect.
- Non-firing products such as "cold glazes" are now stocked by ceramic suppliers. They are used to decorate and restore ceramics and can be applied to glazed and unglazed surfaces. Some need to be hardened in a domestic oven, but a kiln is not necessary.
- Many forms of household paint can be applied to a ceramic surface, but some will wear badly and flake or peel and are not recommended for outdoor situations. Paint will key to a porous surface much more permanently than to a glazed one, and may prove useful for sculptural applications. Washes of acrylic paint are especially durable on biscuit, and car spray paint is also very tough.

Right: A collection of pots in mixed stoneware clay, by Aki Moriuchi. Gritblasting is used to create a highly unusual, distressed surface reminiscent of ancient pots found on a sea-bed. Glazes are applied on biscuit in layers (usually 10–12 different glazes). After the first glaze—firing and blasting—pots are re-glazed and re-fired where necessary.

Gritblasting Using Resists

SANDBLASTING IS THE NAME formerly given to gritblasting and is still in common use. Sand is no longer used due to the health hazards caused by silica dust, and now abrasive aluminum oxides/silicates or iron silicates are used instead. Blasting is simple, but it relies on specialized equipment, and its use by studio potters is relatively recent. Gritblasting equipment is costly but can be found in some art schools, especially in glass departments. A gritblaster consists of a cabinet in which the work is placed, held by protective gloves from outside (*see page 147*) while abrasive grit is blasted at the surface of the work. Depending on the pressure and the length of time the gun is used, the surface becomes first matte and abraded, then erodes considerably. Softer, low-fired clays are worn more quickly than high-fired ones. Gritblasting is effective in conjunction with a resist, showing a contrast between protected and blasted areas. Here we demonstrate the use of three different types of resist. A good dust mask should be worn at all times when griblasting.

YOU WILL NEED
Gritblasting facilities
Glazed tiles or other work
Electrical tape, Latex, or wood glue

TAPE RESIST

1 A commercial tile, glazed with earthenware gloss blue, is covered with resistive tape—broad electrical tape is the preferred choice. Strips of tape are cut through and peeled away to allow the grit to abrade the surface in those areas.

2 After light gritblasting, the tape is removed to reveal faint abrasion, just enough to frost the surface and make the glaze matte. The contrast is subtle.

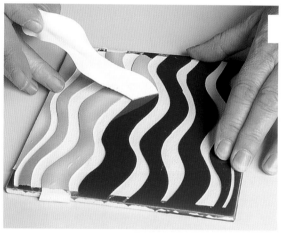

3 A similar tile subjected to heavier gritblasting, which cut through the glaze completely and revealed the clay beneath. The effect is more dramatic, and the surface has a ridged texture.

↑ The finished tile, with a pink stain rubbed into the porous background clay.

VARIATIONS

Left and center: *Ring-tailed Lemur jar and Tiger bowl. Both in sandblasted porcelain and fired to 2282°F (1250°C) in an oxidizing atmosphere.* DIMITRI GRIVELLIS

Right: *Biscuit fired tiles were coated with a mixture of red iron oxide and wallpaper paste, then fired. Tape was used as a resist to protect the oxide surface before blasting. Blasting has removed the oxide coating in areas leaving raised leaf shapes against a biscuit background.* LES RUCINSKI

Far right: *A biscuit fired piece was trailed and dotted with latex, which was then allowed to dry before being blasted. Before the latex was removed the piece was glazed with a copper-stained matte barium glaze. The latex was removed and the bowl was fired to 2102°F (1150°C).* JO CONNELL

LATEX RESIST

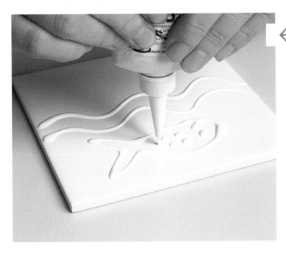

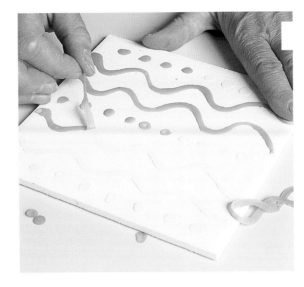

1 Latex is trailed on a biscuit-fired (unglazed) tile to act as a resist. It gives fluid lines similar to slip trailing. Latex does not adhere well to glazed ware, and must dry completely before blasting.

2 The latex is removed from the tile after blasting. The effect is subtle and textural. It could now be glazed, if wished. This method can be used on any porous, fired ware.

This pattern too was created with a white (PVA) glue resist. After blasting the unresisted part of the tile is porous, because blasting removes the glaze. A wash of underglaze color was applied and fired on to subtle effect.

WHITE (PVA) GLUE AS RESIST

← A third resist technique uses white (PVA) wood glue—a good resist for a glazed surface. Again it must dry completely, which could take several hours. After blasting the resist will wash off in warm water.

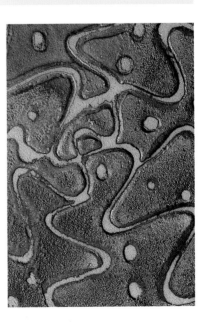

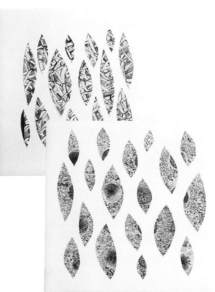

Weathering Effects

CLAY IS EASILY ERODED. At the dry stage it will be affected rapidly by gritblasting, but will create a lot of fine dust. At the biscuit stage too, it will be soft enough to erode quickly. Higher fired or glazed work will take more effort, but will erode in a more controllable way. It is very easy to overdo gritblasting and end up with a pile of dust, so proceed with caution to begin with. Clay can also be affected by controlled natural weathering, though this will require more patience!

BEFORE AND AFTER EFFECTS

↑ This half-blasted head demonstrates the before-and-after effect of gritblasting. Much of the detail is lost and a weathered effect is achieved.

↑ Half-weathered panel. A resist was used to protect one half, showing the comparative effect of erosion by gritblasting.

↑ Peter Hayes is seen here putting one of his raku-fired pieces into the sea, where an interesting weathering process takes place. After firing, any cracks or textured surfaces are filled with a paste using copper metal powder. The sea salts oxidize the copper into copper verdigris. The longer it is kept in the sea, the more the copper transports through the clay body giving a turquoise blush.

VARIATIONS

Left: Small head, blasted before applying red iron oxide. GABRIELLE RUCINSKI
Center: "Bowl of Dry Water." Mixed stoneware clays were thrown and altered. The piece was fired in a gas kiln in an oxidizing atmosphere, and then gritblasted. AKI MORIUCHI
Right: Weathered shoe, biscuit fired and gritblasted. GABRIELLE RUCINSKI

Metal Leaf

METAL LEAF CAN ADD a "precious" touch to a finished piece, and can usually be found in the catalogs of sculptors' and artists' suppliers. It is available as copper, silver, gold, or gold substitute. The leaf comes in books, as loose leaf, or as transfer leaf with a paper backing. It is featherlight and disintegrates readily. The transfer leaf is easier to handle, though not suitable for all purposes. This sequence shows the use of gold transfer leaf on a fired raku piece.

Gold leaf needs no surface protection, though beeswax can be used to soften its brightness. Copper needs varnish to prevent tarnishing—good acrylic varnishes are suitable. Silver leaf can be patinated with potassium sulfide to give an aged effect.

YOU WILL NEED

Metal leaf
Gold size
Soft brush
Suitable finished work to apply it to

Examples of metal leaf (left to right): gold and copper loose leaf; transfer silver leaf.

1 Prepare the surface to accept the gold leaf with a special glue, known as "gold size."

2 Position the gold leaf transfer, holding the overhanging transfer paper, and then rub with the fingers to make sure it adheres well.

3 The transfer paper peels off easily, leaving the gold in place. Gaps can be filled with extra gold leaf if required, but the fragmented appearance gives character here, and is suited to this textured surface.

151

The finished piece: a raku-fired form with textured surface and gold leaf, by Heather Morris.

VARIATIONS

Below: *Smoke-fired stoneware platters with gold leaf.* JOY BOSWORTH
Right: *Terra cotta clay, relief printed from plaster mold, fired to 2102°F (1150°C), then enhanced with gold leaf.* HEATHER MORRIS

Mixed Media

THE USE OF REPEATED FIRINGS, assembling a variety of ceramic pieces or combining materials, can take ceramics farther into the arena of fine art and sculpture. Just as ceramics can imitate many different surfaces it can also complement and be enhanced by other materials. Fired clay can appear hard and metallic, or soft and yielding, responding to both man made and natural forms.

In practical terms it is important to remember that clay will shrink as it is fired. Furthermore, some form of attachment should be planned as part of the making process so that the addition of another material appears considered rather than an afterthought. In the examples shown here we see enhancement of clay at the final stage and the innovative use of other media as contrasting additions to ceramic in its various guises. Borrowing from other art forms and craft processes offers numerous possibilities for future development, with tremendous scope for adding another dimension to the ceramic process. A ceramic piece is not finished until the maker decides it is!

↑ The wooliness of sheep is fully expressed in this wall-hung sculpture made by ceramicist Jan Beeny and textile artist Kathy Williams. Both artists have expressed their craft and combined their skills to great effect.

← Essentially a salt-glaze potter, Steve Harrison incorporates other materials into his work in the form of silver or hardwood knobs and spouts as contrasting elements in a formal design.

← This stoneware balloon bowl by Monica Sinclair Smith introduces mixed media in an unusual form. Colorful balloons protrude through pierced holes to provide an exciting contrast. Ceramics moves into a party mood.

A combination of glass and ceramics by Giovanna Nicklin. → Porcelain pieces, incised and underglaze colored, are combined with strips made by fusing crushed, colored glass between sheets of window glass. The edges are copper-foiled.

← Saggar-fired, mixed-media assemblages by Rebecca Green. After biscuit firing, these pieces are fired in a saggar along with vegetable peelings, sawdust, copper carbonate, magnesium carbonate, and salt to create an aged, decayed appearance.

↑ One of a series of flying fish by Rosamonde Ingham, which bring together flotsam and jetsum in the form of found objects with vividly glazed ceramic fish components to make exciting hanging sculptures.

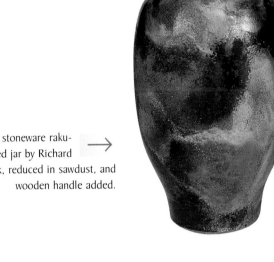

Thrown stoneware raku-fired jar by Richard Capstick, reduced in sawdust, and wooden handle added.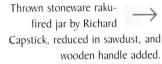

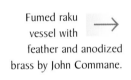

Fumed raku vessel with feather and anodized brass by John Commane.

Thrown and altered stoneware bowl with metal-handled spoon by John Commane. →

Raku light in crank clay by Richard Capstick. Hand built, raku fired, and reduced in sawdust. Finished with glass. ←

The hardness of sprung forged iron handles combines with glossy porcelain, and a surface twist echoes throughout these forms by Joanna Howells. →

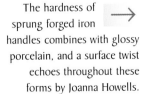

HEALTH AND SAFETY

It is important to observe a "common sense" safety code when making and firing ceramics, so please read and follow this advice on workshop practice.

HAZARDOUS SUBSTANCES

Some materials are toxic and must be handled with caution. All materials should be labeled by your supplier, who will also be able to provide data sheets about them. Follow manufacturers' recommendations for use and storage.

Damaged packages should always be rebagged, and dry materials preferably kept in a sealed plastic container—avoid the use of glass jars in the workshop. Keep bags and containers sealed when not in use, and always use a scoop.

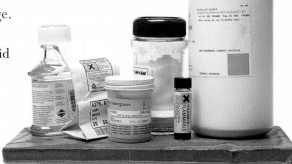

DUST

Dust is probably the biggest hazard in the pottery studio. Some materials are toxic and must not be inhaled or ingested, but even clay dust is a problem. Particles of silica in clay are so tiny that they can bypass all filtering systems in the nose and throat, and settle in the lungs, causing irreversible damage. For this reason, be sure to heed the following:

PROTECTIVE CLOTHING

• Preferred protective clothing is polyester, which does not hold the dust as much as natural fabrics. Wash your clothing clean regularly.

• Always wear a mask when doing "dusty" jobs, such as glaze mixing, fettling dry clay, or gritblasting.

Dust mask

• When spraying ceramic materials, wear a respiratory mask, and check efficiency of extraction equipment regularly. Wet back spray booths, now in common use, are even more user-friendly.

WORKSHOP PRACTICE

• Clean up immediately when spillages happen—don't leave them to dry.

• Keep benches, walls, and floors clean by wet-wiping or mopping rather than brushing.

• Clean potters are healthy potters. Never eat, drink, or smoke in the workshop.

Respirator

ELECTRICITY

- Do not get water on electric motors or switches and make sure hands are dry.

- Machinery sometimes has a guard fitted. Never remove guards or operate machinery with the outer casing removed.

- Electric wiring is a job for an electrician. Never be tempted to do it yourself. All mains-powered equipment is potentially dangerous if wired up incorrectly.

KILNS

- Gas kilns: be sure to have a "flame failure" device fitted to the burners to avoid the risk of explosion.

- Make sure there are no combustible materials near the kiln when it is in use.

- Fumes emitted during firing can be harmful when inhaled. Enamels, lusters, covercoat, and some mediums give off especially noxious fumes. An adequate extraction facility must be installed, and if possible a kiln should be located in a separate room from the workshop.

RAKU

- Do not use any kind of flammable solvents with a low flashpoint (such as methylated spirits) anywhere near the kiln or reduction chambers.

- Always wear heatproof gauntlets (foundry type) when dealing with the hot kiln, and proper protective shoes—not sandals. Tie hair back and beware of loose clothing.

- A full face visor is recommended for all raku-type activities.

- Beware of smoke inhalation and keep the smoke to a minimum.

- Remember that even though pots may not be glowing red, they can still be hot enough to cause serious burns. Think before you touch.

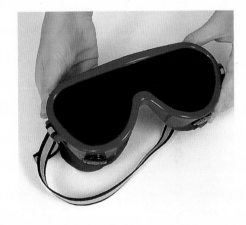

Raku goggles

- When pots are dunked into a bin of sawdust and the lid put in place, it can be dangerous to take the lid off and allow oxygen into the bin until everything has cooled down. A sudden intake of air can cause an explosion and unexpected flames. Some sawdust or shavings are from lumber treated with preservatives and can flare alarmingly.

- See Container Firing (page 116) for additional tips on the safe handling of combustible materials.

Protective gauntlets

Glossary

ASH Useful ingredient as the fluxing agent for a glaze. Wood ash is usual, but coal ash, and any plant ash is also usable. Ash also may have a high silica content, and combined with clay it will form a simple stoneware glaze.

BALL CLAY Clay of high plasticity, high firing and pale in color. An ingredient of throwing clay and other bodies, as well as glazes.

BODY/CLAY BODY Term potters use for clay, especially when it is a prepared mixture and may contain other non-plastic materials such as grog and sand.

BENTONITE A plastic volcanic clay used in small amounts for suspending glazes or increasing the plasticity of a clay body.

BISCUIT (BISQUE) First, low-temperature firing to which a pot is subjected. Moisture within the clay is driven off slowly in the form of steam, along with other organic compounds—clay becomes converted to "pot," a chemical change that is irreversible. Biscuit firing is usually between 1562°F and 1832°F (850°C and 1000° C) but can be higher if less porosity required. Work is often biscuit fired before being decorated in other ways.

CARBORUNDUM STONE A hard, dense stone used for grinding away rough patches on fired ceramic.

CLAY ($Al_2O_3.2SiO_2.2H_2O$) Essentially the product of weathered granite and feldspathic rock; a hydrated silicate of aluminium. The purest "primary" clay, china clay (Kaolin), is found where it was formed. Transported "secondary" clays become contaminated, are colored and due to the variable presence of fluxes have a range of lower firing temperatures.

COBALT OXIDE/CARBONATE (CoO and $CoCO_3$) Powerful blue colorants. Used widely in ancient China, cobalt is said to have been first found in Persia. Blue and white decoration is one of the strongest traditions in ceramics.

CONES/PYROMETRIC CONES Compressed glaze material formulated to bend at designated temperatures. The structures are placed in the kiln where they can be seen through the spy hole. They provide an accurate indicator of the "heat-work" of the firing, i.e. the real effectiveness of temperature and time on the clay and glazes.

COPPER OXIDE/CARBONATE ($CuCO_3$) Strong colorant in ceramics giving green to black and brown. Under certain reduction conditions it can give a blood red.

DEFLOCCULANT An alkaline substance, commonly sodium silicate or soda ash, which when added to a slip, makes the mixture more fluid without the addition of water. The clay particles remain dispersed and in suspension, an essential quality required for casting. Also see Flocculant.

DELFTWARE Also known as Majolica and Faience, this tin-glazed ceramic ware was named after the town of Delft in Holland. (See Majolica, page 88.)

EARTHENWARE Low temperature ceramics generally fired between 1832°F and 2156°F (1000°C and 1180° C). Earthenware pottery is fused but not vitrified and remains porous unless covered with a glaze. Naturally occurring red terra cotta clays have a relatively high iron oxide content that acts as a flux and therefore will not withstand high temperatures. White earthenware is a manufactured clay body used widely for industrial production.

ENGOBE Prepared slip that contains some fluxing ingredient. It lies halfway between a clay slip and a glaze.

FETTLING Term used when cast ware is trimmed and sponged to remove excess clay and seams. Fettling is done at the leatherhard or dry stage.

FIRING Process that changes clay to ceramic (see Biscuit). The usual firing ranges referred to are raku, the lowest at around 1472°F (800°C), followed by earthenware, then stoneware and finally porcelain, which can be fired up to a maximum of 2552°F (1400°C).

FLOCCULANT An acid or salt, which when added to slip has a thickening effect and aids suspension, delaying settlement. Calcium chloride and vinegar are commonly used flocculants.

FLUX An essential glaze ingredient that lowers the melting point of silica, the glass-making ingredient. A number of oxides serve as fluxes, each having its own characteristics.

FRIT Material used in low temperature glazes. Frits are made by heating and fusing certain materials together, after which they are finely ground to a powder. In this way soluble or toxic substances can be stabilized and made safe to use.

FUSED Melted together, but not necessarily vitrified.

GLAZE Super-cooled liquid of glass-like nature that is fused to the surface of a pot. The chemistry of glaze is complex but fascinating.

IRON OXIDE The most common and very versatile coloring oxide, used in many slips and glazes and often present in clays too. Red iron oxide (rust) is the most usual form but there are others (black iron, purple iron, yellow ocher).

JIGGER & JOLLEY Plastic clay is formed on or in a rotating plaster mold with a metal profile. Jolleying produces hollow ware, jiggering produces flatware. Mostly an industrial process, but sometimes used by studio potters.

KAOLIN China clay. Primary clay in its purest form ($Al_2O_3.2SiO_2.2H_2O$).

LEATHERHARD Stage during the drying process at which the clay becomes stiff and no longer pliable, but is still damp. In this state it can be easily handled while retaining its shape.

ONCE FIRING Firing ceramics without a biscuit firing, usually with a raw glaze or pigment applied at the leatherhard or dry stage.

OPACIFIER Material used to make a glaze more opaque, often tin oxide, titanium oxide or zirconium silicate.

PLASTER OF PARIS / PLASTER ($2CaSO_4.H_2O$) A semi-hydrated calcium sulfate, derived from gypsum by driving off part of the water content. Used in moldmaking.

PORCELAIN Highly vitrified white clay body with a high kaolin content. Developed and widely used in ancient China, its low plasticity makes it a difficult clay to work with. It can be fired as high as 2552°F (1400°C) and when thinly formed, the fired body is translucent.

PYROMETER Temperature indicator linked to a kiln via a thermocouple. Pyrometers can be analogue or digital, the latter being preferred by many potters these days.

REFRACTORY Resistant to heat, and in terms of clay, one that can be fired to high temperatures without melting. Kiln bricks and shelves are made from refractory materials

SAGGAR Vessel made of refractory clay used to contain pots during firing. In the ceramics industry, a "saggar maker's bottom knocker" would beat out the clay for the bases of saggars with a kind of flattened wooden mallet.

SOAK Time during the firing cycle when a steady temperature (often the peak) is maintained in the kiln to allow glazes to flow and mature.

SAWDUST FIRING Sawdust is the fuel most often used for smoking or reducing ceramics at low temperatures.

SILICA Silicon Dioxide (SiO_2) Primary glass-forming ingredient used in glazes and also present in clay. Silica does not melt until approximately 3272°F (1800°C) and must always be used in conjunction with a flux to reduce its melting point to a workable temperature range.

SLIP CASTING Casting slip is made from clay and water, but also contains a deflocculant, allowing a reduced water content. Poured into a plaster mold, casting slip is then left to build up a shell on the inside of the mold before pouring out the excess. Remaining moisture is absorbed by the plaster.

STONEWARE Vitrified ceramics fired above 2192°F (1200°C). Stoneware is hard, dense, and waterproof (it has an absorption rate of less than 1 percent).

THROWING Clay is placed on a rotating potter's wheel and formed by hand in conjunction with centrifugal force. Wheel designs vary from momentum "man-powered" wheels, through pedal type "kick wheels" and belt-driven, hand-turned arrangements to the modern highly powered electric version. Throwing is said to have been developed first in Egypt c. 3000 B.C.

TURNING/TRIMMING After throwing, pots are often inverted and put back on the wheel at the leatherhard stage. A metal cutting tool is used to pare off excess, cut details such as footrings, and generally refine the form.

VITRIFICATION Process by which clay materials bond to become dense, impervious and glassified during the latter part of a firing. The resulting pots are hard and durable. The vitrification point is the temperature to which a clay can be fired without deformation. See Stoneware.

WATER-BASED MEDIUM Carrier that allows a pigment to be applied in the desired way. Increasingly, water-based or "water-friendly" mixtures are being used in ceramics, for reasons of convenience and health and safety, and in preference to traditional oil-based materials, which are often rather pungent and are flammable. Various mixtures are available, often based on glycerin, and your supplier will advise on their application.

WEDGING/KNEADING Methods of preparing clay by hand to form a homogenous mix. It mixes clay of uneven texture and removes air pockets. Spiral kneading arranges the platelets in an advantageous way for throwing.

Suppliers

UNITED KINGDOM

LES BAINBRIDGE
The Crescent
Loggerheads
Market Drayton TF9 4PE
Tel: 01630 673762

BATH POTTERS SUPPLIES
2 Dorset Close
Bath BA2 3RF
Tel: 01225 337046
www.bathpotters.demon.co.uk

CHAS LAMB GEOTECHNICS
(for titanium lusters)
39 Farleigh Fields
Orton Wistow
Peterborough PE2 6YB
Tel: 01733 234096

CTM SUPPLIES
9 Spruce Close
Exeter EX4 9JU
Tel: 01395 233077

HERAEUS
Unit A Cinderhill Industrial Estate
Weston Coyney Rd
Longton
Stoke on Trent ST3 5LB
Tel: 01782 599423

POTCLAYS LTD
Brickkiln Lane
Etruria
Stoke-on-Trent ST4 7BP
Tel: 01782 219816

POTTERYCRAFTS
Campbell Road
Stoke on Trent ST4 4ET
Tel: 01782 745000
www.potterycrafts.co.uk

POTTERS CONNECTION
Chadwick Street
Longton
Stoke on Trent ST3 1PJ
Tel: 01782 593054

UNITED STATES

ALPHA CERAMIC SUPPLIES
10170 Croydon Way
Sacramento CA 95827
Tel: 916-361-3611

AMACO
4717 West Sixteenth Street
Indianapolis
Indiana 46222

BIG CERAMIC STORE
463 Miwok Court
Femont, CA 94539
www.bigceramicstore.com

CERAMIC SUPPLY OF NEW YORK
7 Route 46 West
Lodi, New Jersey
Tel: 973-340-3005
http://7ceramic.com

CLAY ART CENTER ONLINE
www.clayartcenteronline.com

DUNCAN ENTERPRISES
5673 E. Shields Avenue
Fresno, CA 93727
Tel: 559-291-4444
www.duncanceramics.com

FERRO CORPORATION
1000 Lakeside Avenue
Cleveland, Ohio 44114-7000

GARE INCORPORATED
165 Rosemont Street
Haverhill, MA 01830
Tel: 978-373-9131. FAX: 978-372-9432

GREAT LAKES CLAY & SUPPLY CO.
120 South Lincoln Avenue
Carpentersville, IL 60110
Tel: 800-258-8796
www.greatclay.com

HAMILL & GILLESPIE INC.
154 South Livingston Avenue
PO Box 104, Livingston, NJ 07039
Tel: 800-454-8846

KICKWHEEL POTTERY SUPPLY
6477 Peachtree Industrial Boulevard
Atlanta, GA 30360
Tel: 800-241-1895
www.kickwheel.com

SHEFFIELD POTTERY
Route 7 Box 399
Sheffield MA 01257
Tel: 888-774-2529
www.sheffield-pottery.com

157

Index

All techniques are illustrated.
Page numbers in *italics* refer to
other information in captions.

159

Credits

Key: b = bottom, t = top, c = center, l = left, r = right

Quarto would like to thank and acknowledge the following for supplying pictures reproduced in this book:
8tr: The Art Archive/Musée du Louvre Paris/Dagli Orti; 8cr: Jeremy Hartley/Panos Pictures; p.147tl Guyson International Limited.

Quarto and the author would also like to thank the following artists for permission to reproduce their work in the gallery sections of this book (where a photographer has been specified, the name appears in brackets):
6tl: Jo Connell; 6tr: Ruth Lyne; 6b: Jenny Hale/Louise Darby; 7t: Jo Connell; 7c: Jo Connell; 7b: Jo Connell; 8cl: Jo Connell; 8bl: Peter Beard (Peter Beard); 8br: Jo Connell; 9tl and r: Jo Connell; 9c: Molly Attrill; 9br: Joy Bosworth (River Studios); 9bl: Fleur Harvey (Alan Hayward); 10: all Jo Connell apart from cr: Dawn Kyra Harbord; br: Rosemary Cochrane; bc: Lisa Hammond; 11t: Peter Hayes; 11c: Janet Halligan (M.W. Halligan); 11cr: Jonathan Chiswell Jones; 11br: Jo Connell; 11bl: Penkridge Ceramics; 12tl: Mal Magson; 12tc: Sue Dyer; 12tr: Gerry Unsworth; 13tl: Sue Dyer; 13tc: Peter Ilsley; 13tr: Jo Connell; 13cl: Jo Connell; 13c: Paul Young; 13cl: Lorraine Richardson; 13bc: Lorraine Richardson; 13br: Paul Young; 14t: Ruth Lyne; 14c: Frank Smith; 14b: Anne Brodie; 15c: John Commane; 16b and bc: Ruth Lyne; 16br: Sarah Leyman; 17c: Ruth Lyne; 17br: David Binns; 18t and c: Susan Nemeth (Stephen Brayne); 18b: Sabina Teuteberg (Steve Bryne); 20l: Jack Docherty; 20c: Bridget Aldridge; 20r: Reg Moon; 21l: Les Rucinski; 21r: Bridget Aldridge; 22: All Jo Connell; 23bl: Mal Magson; 23t and br: Jo Connell; 24t: Nigel Edmondson; 24c: Joanna Howells; (Martin Avery); 24b: May Ling Beadsmoore; 24c: David Binns; 25c: Andrew Mason; 25bl: Carlos Van Reisburg Versluys; 25r: Jan Beeny; 26bl: May Ling Beadsmoore; 26br: Andrew Mason; 27bl: Nigel Edmondson; 27br: Louise Darby; 28b: Jonathan Garrett; 29bl: Jo Connell; 29bc: Jonathan Garrett; 29c: Les Rucinski; 29br: Jo Connell; 30b: Louise Darby; 31bl: Jo Connell; 31bc: Frank Smith; 31br: Andrew Cox; 32bl: Les Rucinksi; 32br: Jim Malone; 33cr: Christine Geddes; 33br: Rosemary Cochran; 34bl: Jo Connell; 34bc: Steve Taylor; 34br: John Commane; 35bl: Antonia Salmon; 35bc: Ardine Spitters; 35br: Lorraine Richardson; 36t: Les Rucinksi; 36c: Edward Pooley; 36b: Sarah Monk; 37t: Jo Connell; 37b: Ruth Barker; 38b: Edward Pooley; 39bl: Whichford Pottery; 39br: Jo Connell; 40b: Jo Connell; 40cr: Paul Young; 41bl: Steve Mattison; 41br: Sarah Monk (John Meredith); 42bl: Heather Morris; 42br: Laura Vickers; 43bl: Christine Geddes; 43cr: Les Rucinski; 43br: Juliette Goddard (Juliette Goddard); 44t: Fleur Harvey; 44c: Jude Jelfs; 44b: Christy Keeny; 45bc: Sue Dyer; 45br: Fiona Thompson; 46bl: Jean Paul Landreau; 46bc: Vivienne Ross; 46br: Jude Jelfs; 47c: Jean Paul Landreau; 48br: Carol Wheeler; 49bl: Jo Connell; 49bc: Jo Connell; 49br: Fiona Thompson; 50: Heather Morris; 51br: Sue Dyer; 52tr: Carol Wheeler; 53bl: Jo Connell; 53br: Fleur Harvey; 54t: Caroline Whyman (Caroline Whyman); 54c: Jonna Behrens; 54b: Mark Dally (Mark Dally); 54br: Kochevet Ben-David (Heini Schneible); 55tl: John Calver; 55br: Ralph Jandrell; 56bl: Nick Somerville; 56br: John Commane; 57bl: Paul Young; 57bc: Molly Attrill; 57br: Derek Emms; 58bl: Paul Young; 58br: Kochevet Ben-David (Heini Schneible); 59bl: Mark Dally (Mark Dally); 59bc: Niek Hoogland; 59br: Willi Singleton; 60bl: Paul Young; 60br: Molly Attrill; 61br: 61c: Paul Young; Gabrielle Rucinski; 62bl: Jean Paul Landreau; 62bc: Jo Connell; 62br: Molly Attrill; 63bl and c: John Commane; 64tr: Paul Young; 64b: Jonna Behrens; 65br: John Commane; 66bl: Jo Connell; 66br: Alex McErlain; 67bl: Michael Casson; 67bc and r: Willi Singleton; 68bl: Christine Geddes; 68br: Dominique Keeling; 69cl: Francoise Dufayard; 69cr and br: Molly Attrill; 70: Boscastle Pottery; 71c: Peter Ilsley; 72br: Peter Illsley; 73br: Jo Connell; 74bl: Sue Dyer; 74bl: Caroline Whyman (Caroline Whyman); 75bl: Nicholas Homoky (Nicholas Homoky); 75br: Sue Dyer; 76bl: Willi Singleton; 76br: Jill Fanshawe Kato; 77bl: Chrisine Geddes; 77bc: Jo Connell; 77br: Gerry Unsworth; 78tl: Annette Bridges; 78tc: Carol Peevor; 78tr: Katrina Pechal; 79tl: Bridget Aldridge; 79tc: Jo Connell; 79tr: Ashley Howard; 79cl: Fran Tristram (Rod Bailey); 79c: Steve Harrison (Patrick Harrison); 79cr: Peter Ilsley; 79bl: Janet Hamer (Janet Hamer); 79bc: Paul Young; 79br: Lorraine Richardson; 80t: Anna Lambert; 80c: Roger Lewis; 80b: Brian Ashley; 81c: Nicholas Mosse; 82b: Paul Scott; 83bl: Jan Bunyan; 83bc: Bennett Cooper; 83br: Karen Woolf; 84bl: Jan Bunyan; 85bl: Nicholas Mosse; 85bc: Lorraine Richardson; 86t: Victoria Hughes (Victoria Hughes); 86c: Ashley Howard (Stephen Brayne); 86b: Katrina Pechal; 87bl: Ashley Howard; 87bc: Fran Tristram (Rod Bailey); 87br: John Jelfs (John Jelfs) 88bl: Andrew McGarva; 88br: Alan Caiger Smith/Louise Darby; 89bl: Thunig Pottery; 89bc: Victoria Hughes (Victoria Hughes); 89br: Molly Attrill; 89cr: Lorraine Richardson; 90bl: Gerry Unsworth; 90bc: John Commane; 90cr: Gerry Unsworth; 90br: Jo Connell; 91bl: John Commane; 91bc: Jo Connell; 92br: Fran Tristram (Rod Bailey); 92cl: Clive Davies; 92c: Karen Ann Wood; 92b: Bronwyn Williams Ellis (Bronwyn Williams Ellis); 93bl: Andrew Mason; 93bc: Caroline Genders; 93bl: Peter Beard (Peter Beard); 94cl: Annette Bridges; 94br: Bridget Aldridge; 95tl: Paul Young; 95tr: Andrew Matheson; 95bc: Ashley Howard; 95br:

Katrina Pechal; 96: Christy Keeny; 97cl: Carol Peevor; 97bl: Seth Draper; 97bc: Hans Coper/Louise Darby; 97br: Carol Peevor; 98t: Joanna Howells (Martin Avery); 98c: Emili Biarnes Rabier; 98b: John Calver; 99tl: Kate Malone (Peter Chatterton); 99tr: Steve Harrison; 99bl: Steve Harrison (Patrick Harrison); 99br: Steve Mills; 100bl: Andrew Hemus; 100br: Derek Emms; 101tr: Joanna Howells (Martin Avery); 101c: Mike Reynolds; 101br: Jill Fanshawe Kato; 103bl: Jonathan Chiswell Jones; 103bc: Paul Spence; 103br: Janet Hamer (Janet Hamer); 104bl: Rosemary Cochrane; 104br: Walter Keeler/Louise Darby; 105bl: May Ling Beadsmoore; 105bc: Rosemary Cochrane; 105cr: May Ling Beadsmoore; 105br: Lisa Hammond; 107bl: Peter Ilsley; 107bc and r: Kate Malone (Peter Chatterton); 108tl: Claire Botterill; 108tc: Stephen Murfitt; 108tr: June Taylor; 109tl: Gordon Thomas; 109tc: Jerry Caplan; 109tl: Tony Blenkinsopp; 109cl: Elizabeth Michl; 109c: Christine Gittins; 109cr: June Taylor; 109bl: Bridget Aldridge; 109bc: Clive Oates; 109br: Jo Connell; 110t: Geoff Townsend; 110c: Jaqui Atkin; 110b: Ardine Spitters; 110br:Tessa Wolfe Murray; 111t: Ardine Spitters; 111bl: Christine Gittins; 111br: Elizabeth Michl; 112bl: Elizabeth Michl; 112br: Ardine Spitters; 113bl: Ardine Spitters; 113br: Tamasine Holman (Tamasine Holman); 114bl: Gerry Unsworth; 114bc and r: Christine Gittins: 115: Bridget Aldridge; 117bl and r: June Taylor; 117c: Geoff Townsend; 117tr: Sebastian Blackie; 118br: John Commane; 119bl: Jo Connell; 119bc and r: John Commane; 120t: Mervyn Nichol (Mervyn Nichol); 120c: Jo Connell; 120b: Tony White; 120br: Stephen Murfitt; 121c: Clive Oates; 122–123l to r: Stephen Murfitt (Terry Beard); 122bl: Richard Capstick; 122br: Jo Connell; 123bl: Gordon Thomas; 123br: Tony White; 124bl: Jo Connell; 124br: Jerry Caplan; 125tr: Tony Blenkinsopp; 125br: Jo Connell; 126-127: Tony Blenkinsopp; 127bl: John Commane; 127bc: David Roberts; 127br: Heather Morris; 128b: Mervyn Nichol (Mervyn Nichol); 129cr: Tony Blenkinsopp; 129bl: Clive Oates; 129bc: Claire Botterill; 129bx: Harry Dancey; 130tl: Will Levi Marshall; 130tc: Monica Sinclair Smith; 130tr: Heather Morris; 131tl: Philomena Pretsell (John McKenzie); 131cl: John Commane; 131cl: Stephanie Redfern; 131cl: Dimitra Grivellis (Stephen Brayne); 131cl: Heather Morris; 131br: Maria Stewart; 131bc: David MacGregor; 131br: Anne James; 132t: Andrew Docherty; 132c: Stephanie Redfern; 132b: Philomena Pretsell (John McKenzie); 132br: Laura Vickers; 133tr: Will Levi Marshall; 133bl: Virginia Graham; 134: Stephanie Redfern; 135bl: Malcolm Unsworth; 146cr: Jo Connell; 136bl: Ken Whittingham; 137: All Jo Connell; 139br: Will Levi Marshall; 140t: Mary Rich; 140c: Gerry Unsworth; 140br: Philomena Pretsell (John McKenzie); 141c and b: David MacGregor; 142bl: Gerry Unsworth; 142br: Les Rucinski; 143c: Maria Stewart; 143bl: Mary Rich; 143bc: Gerry Unsworth; 143br: Les Rucinski; 144br: Anne James; 144bl: Gerry Unsworth; 145bc and r: John Wheeldon; 146t: Peter Beard (Peter Beard); 146c: Joy Bosworth (River Studios); 146bl and r: Dimitra Grivellis (Stephen Brayne); 146br: Aki Moriuchi; 148b and 149bl: Dimitra Grivellis (Stephen Brayne); 149bc: Les Rucinski; 149br: Jo Connell; 150bl and r: Gabrielle Rucinski; 150c: Aki Moriuchi; 151l: Heather Morris; 151bc: Joy Bosworth (River Studios); 151br: Heather Morris; 152tl: Steve Harrison (Patrick Harrison); 152tr: Jan Beeny/Kathy Williams (Jan Beeny); 152c: Monica Sinclair Smith; 152br: Giovanna Nicklin; 152bl: Rebecca Green; 153tl: Rosamonde Ingram; 153tr: Richard Capstick; 153cl and r: John Commane; 153bl: Richard Capstick; 153br: Joanna Howells (Abbas Nazari).

All other photographs and illustrations are the copyright of Quarto. While every effort has been made to credit contributors, we apologize should there have been any omissions or errors.

Author's Acknowledgments
I am very much indebted to the many people who helped with this book. The following people willingly shared their expertise by demonstrating various skills and techniques in front of the camera:
Bridget Aldridge, Tony Blenkinsopp, Jan Bunyan, John Commane, Louise Darby, Sue Dyer, Janet Hamer, Peter Ilsley, Ruth Lyne, Heather Morris, Carol Peevor, Edward Pooley, Stephanie Redfern, Lorraine Richardson, Les Rucinski, Frank Smith, Maria Stewart, June Taylor, Gerry Unsworth, Malcolm Unsworth, Carol Wheeler, Ken Whittingham, Paul Young.

Many photographs were taken by the author. Material for photography was provided by many others, amongst whom the following deserve special mention: Sebastian Blackie, Rosemary Cochrane, DBS (Midlands) Ltd, Elizabeth Michl, Andrew Matheson, North Warwickshire & Hinckley College, Gill Pemberton, Mike Reynolds, Thompson Evans Collection.
   Very many thanks to the numerous potters who contributed photographs of their work. These have enriched and enlivened the book, illustrating the wealth and breadth of creativity and professionalism which characterizes today's studio ceramics scene.

Special thanks to John Commane for his help in the studio and to Rosemary Cochrane for added inspiration. Most of all, thanks to my husband John for his immense patience and support, both moral and technical.